Alexandria

Rediscovered

View of Alexandria from a helicopter. The shot was taken from the north across the Eastern Harbour. One can see Qait Bey Fort part of the way along the western breakwater. On the right, behind the beginning of the Western Harbour, one can see the waters of Lake Mariut.

OVERLEAF: The Eastern Harbour consists of a large basin: this was the Megas Limen, or Great Harbour, of antiquity. Today, as if frozen in time since the Graeco-Roman period, it provides an anchorage for fishing boats, while large commercial vessels only use the Western Harbour.

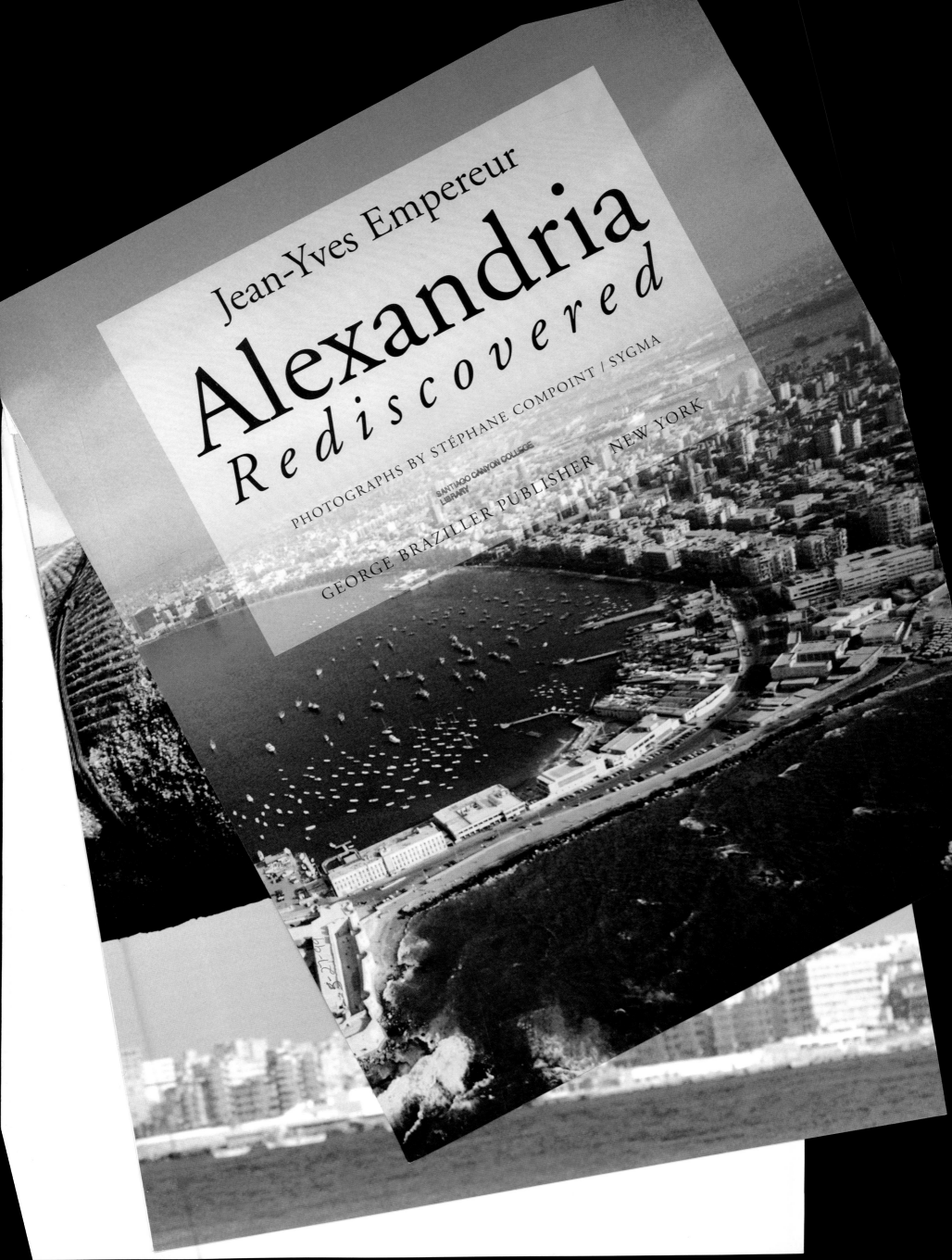

Jean-Yves Empereur

Alexandria
Rediscovered

PHOTOGRAPHS BY STÉPHANE COMPOINT / SYGMA

GEORGE BRAZILLER PUBLISHER · NEW YORK

T HIS BOOK IS A RESPONSE to the frequent requests I have received to publish a preliminary assessment of my experiences as an archaeologist in Alexandria in the form of a work accessible to the wider public. Its aim is not to relate the history of the Ptolemies' capital, but simply to show how a few years spent on its site have made it possible to shed new light on certain problems concerning the topography of the ancient city.

Alexandria is, of course, known to us through numerous literary sources, since many ancient authors visited the 'megalopolis' of the Hellenistic world, or at least wrote about it. Some of them spent time there, like the geographer Strabo, and his description of the city will be one of those most frequently mentioned in the following pages. Others, like Cicero, never went there but often mention it: in his case one can talk of a real obsession with Alexandria – to such a degree that one could even contemplate writing a description of the city under the last Ptolemies based on his works!

Some descriptions of its monuments have been handed down to us. In around AD 40 Philo of Alexandria gives us an impression of the Caesareum, a sanctuary which in his time was still relatively

Cemetery of Anfushi. On the walls, above a high plinth imitating alabaster, a chequerboard pattern is painted in black and white, leaving two panels free on which pharaonic crowns are depicted. On the ceiling is a painted pattern of yellow tiles. All these tombs, hollowed out of Alexandria's limestone rock, imitate the architecture of buildings.

new: it had been begun by Cleopatra in honour of Mark Antony and finished after their deaths in 30 BC by Octavian (later styled Augustus), under whom it had become a shrine dedicated to the imperial family. Philo's text, however, is rather vague: he goes into raptures over the beauty of the building but does not even tell us to what architectural order it belonged, or give us any details about its construction. Other sources are more specific, for instance the description given by Rufinus of the sanctuary of Sarapis at the end of the fourth century AD (see pp. 92–5). Such late works have, however, been suspected of being unreliable: Rufinus may not even have seen this temple before its destruction in AD 391, and, as a Christian propagandist, he is biased in what he selects from the information on pagan cults that he is passing on.

Nevertheless, these authors do at least still furnish us with descriptions we can make use of. There were indeed many others who wrote whole monographs on the city, or rather on its monuments, but the loss of the literature of the ancient world has left us with no more than their titles. The main body of these works fell victim to the fires which ravaged the libraries of Alexandria.

The result is that we have the names of a series of edifices, but know next to nothing about their appearance and location. Like St John Chrysostomos, we can continue to marvel at the bad memory of the Alexandrians: he was asking himself back in the fourth century where the tomb of Alexander could be, and in spite of the 140 or so attempts made since the nineteenth century to locate it, we can still repeat his question today: where was the last resting place of the city's founder?

We should not be tempted to compare the remains of Alexandria with those of Rome, whose leaders were often obsessed with the possible threat Alexandria presented to their power. Nowadays, one can wander through Rome and buy a ticket to visit Augustus' mausoleum, or walk around in Hadrian's Pantheon, and then discover Pompey's theatre in the middle of a stately *palazzo*. In Alexandria nothing of this sort is possible. The last traces of the city's splendour disappeared only recently, almost as if, conforming to the will of its Roman conqueror after hundreds of years, people had felt compelled systematically to denude the Ptolemies' capital, to punish it for having made its rival on the Tiber tremble. Even our near-contemporaries contributed to this denudation by removing the two obelisks of Tuthmosis III ('Cleopatra's Needles') which marked the entrance to the Caesareum. It is only just over a century ago that sailors came from overseas to transport them from the site they had graced for almost two millennia, one to the banks of the Thames, the other to Manhattan.

As for the excavations in the city's bowels, they tell the story of the death-throes of the ancient city, unable to withstand the blows inflicted upon it by the living. Compared with the handful of sites which can be viewed today, so many monuments have disappeared for good, despite the dedication and enthusiasm of the archaeologists who have succeeded one another as directors of the Graeco-Roman Museum. Italians, English and then Egyptians, they have shown a genuine passion for their city, but it has been a losing battle, and one is forced to confess that the situation is getting worse: the move to remodel the city centre, which is making Alexandria one of the major urban conglomerations of the Mediterranean, involves irreversible sacrifices – and the pace is quickening. In the last forty to fifty years, not a single archaeological site has been preserved: that at Kom el-Dikka was the

This funerary couch is in a large hypogeum in the necropolis of Mustafa Kamal, more than three kilometres (2 miles) to the east of the city walls. It was here that the Italian archaeologist Adriani uncovered a series of tombs with monumental architecture, dating from the third and second centuries BC. The frame of the couch and its two stone cushions are painted. A similar couch has just been found in the excavations in the necropolis of Gabbari.

Mustafa Kamal: a view of the tomb in which the painted couch in the preceding photograph was discovered. We are in the main chapel facing the atrium, the only room open to the sky. On the right, three rows of *loculi*, one above the other, can be made out. In the foreground, between two pairs of Doric columns, is the antechamber of the burial chamber proper.

last. It was saved at the beginning of the 1960s and then excavated expertly and systematically by a Polish team. It is the city centre's green lung; far from being a blot on the landscape, it has become a tourist attraction which draws thousands of visitors every year. One can only regret that this example has not been followed.

The defeat of archaeology at Alexandria is by no means due to natural conditions: its causes are human. Foreign archaeologists paid visits to the city during the nineteenth century, but they were all too brief. They thought that they would quickly find the city's principal monuments, starting, obviously, with Alexander's tomb. One can imagine how disheartened these westerners were, especially Heinrich Schliemann, who had had such success at Mycenae and Troy in the 1870s and 1880s. Their slogan was, 'There is nothing to hope for at Alexandria; you classical archaeologists, who have found so much in Greece or in Asia Minor, forget this city.' This was the message of the English archaeologist D.G. Hogarth after an unproductive

expedition in the 1890s. Naturally, his colleagues got the message, and the exploration of the ancient city was directed by local archaeologists with limited means and by civil servants directly answerable to the hierarchic local administration. In spite of their enthusiasm, they must often have found themselves torn between their loyalty to the administration and their respect for the objects it was their duty to save. I must confess I would have found such constraints impossibly frustrating.

This is why the part of the ancient city we know best is the ancient cemeteries, which lay outside the walls and which were discovered as the result of construction projects only after the city centre had become too built-up to permit effective intervention by the Archaeological Service, which came into existence in the 1890s, around fifty years after the development of the modern city had started to gain momentum.

Over the past century, the increase in our knowledge of Alexandrian archaeology has been only modest. Despite the efforts of such outstanding

Mustafa Kamal: the tomb next door to the preceding one. We are in the open-air atrium: in the centre is an altar for the sacrifices performed in honour of the dead; in the background, doorways guarded by three pairs of little sphinxes lead into the burial chambers. Between the Doric columns, a painted panel shows a Macedonian horseman in three-quarter view in a scene that is clearly the work of a talented artist.

BELOW: In one of the Anfushi tombs, a chapel is decorated with alternating palm trees and olive trees (or possibly sycomore-fig trees).

RIGHT: A wholly pharaonic scene is painted on the stairwell of another of the Anfushi tombs (second century BC).

figures as Botti, Breccia, Adriani, Rowe and Rodziewicz, most of the monuments mentioned in the ancient sources are for us still only names without any trace of physical remains. It is as if these buildings were suspended in the air above the map, waiting for us to find a clue that would enable them to land.

Moreover, the physical conditions have not always made the archaeologists' work easy. The ancient strata lie deeply buried, often below the water-table, the level of which has risen as a result of the subsidence that has profoundly affected the area. One frequently has to dig down ten metres (32 ft) or more to reach the installations of Alexandria's first citizens.

In view of these gaps in our knowledge, I felt that I could present this book neither as a guide to the ancient city nor as a historical survey based on the ancient texts: many such works have been written already. While it is true that it has been possible to save a certain number of sites, in spite of the obstacles mentioned above, it seemed to me preferable to illustrate the future hopes of Alexandrian archaeology from my own experience.

I shall mention only for the record the remains visible today. A good

example is the group of cemeteries, preserved by chance, that presents us with an unbroken chronological sequence of burials. The earliest, that of Shatby, with its hypogea (rock-cut tombs) surmounted by above-ground funerary monuments, goes back to the first generations of Alexandrians.

Next in chronological order are the hypogea of Mustafa Kamal, which provide examples of monumental tombs in the Doric style with painted decoration that in certain ways recalls that of the royal tombs of the Macedonian rulers at Vergina. One has a scene depicting a cavalryman seen in three-quarter view; another a carved stone couch with richly decorated cushions. Everything here evokes the world of the Greeks who came to Egypt with Alexander or with his officer Ptolemy, the future master of the country.

The cemetery of Anfushi on the former island of Pharos contains in its turn burials dating from the second and first centuries BC. Here one sees underground tombs with Egyptian scenes which demonstrate the assimilation of the Egyptians' religion by the Greeks of Alexandria.

Some sites present a remarkable continuity throughout the three centuries of the Hellenistic period. The first century AD, meanwhile, is represented by the catacombs of Kom el-Shuqafa, which I shall discuss in detail, as the Centre for Alexandrian Studies (Centre d'Etudes Alexandrines: CEA) has been working on them. I shall also be mentioning the houses of the Alexandrians, their necropoleis and certain important buildings such as the Pharos lighthouse or the Caesareum in connection with the excavations I have been able to undertake in the course of the last ten years.

For everything else – be it literary sources or archaeological sites which have been reported on elsewhere – the reader is advised to refer to existing works on the capital of the Ptolemies. Undoubtedly the best of these is still P. M. Fraser's *Ptolemaic Alexandria* (1972), supplemented by Christoph Haas' *Alexandria in Late Antiquity* (1997).

This tomb was discovered in the east of the city by Adriani, in Tigranes Pasha Street (now Port Said Street). Its wall-paintings, which were removed to save them from the developers, are now in the garden of the archaeological site of the Kom el-Shuqafa catacombs. This naive painting dates from the end of the first century AD. On the corridor wall can be seen a pharaoh and, above him, the Apis bull. In the chapel, above one of the three sarcophagi in the room, Osiris is shown being mummified. The other scenes represent the resurrection and the adoration of Osiris. The ceiling is in Greek style: a Medusa head surrounded by felines chasing cervids.

example is the group of cemeteries, preserved by chance, that presents us with an unbroken chronological sequence of burials. The earliest, that of Shatby, with its hypogea (rock-cut tombs) surmounted by above-ground funerary monuments, goes back to the first generations of Alexandrians.

Next in chronological order are the hypogea of Mustafa Kamal, which provide examples of monumental tombs in the Doric style with painted decoration that in certain ways recalls that of the royal tombs of the Macedonian rulers at Vergina. One has a scene depicting a cavalryman seen in three-quarter view; another a carved stone couch with richly decorated cushions. Everything here evokes the world of the Greeks who came to Egypt with Alexander or with his officer Ptolemy, the future master of the country.

The cemetery of Anfushi on the former island of Pharos contains in its turn burials dating from the second and first centuries BC. Here one sees underground tombs with Egyptian scenes which demonstrate the assimilation of the Egyptians' religion by the Greeks of Alexandria.

Some sites present a remarkable continuity throughout the three centuries of the Hellenistic period. The first century AD, meanwhile, is represented by the catacombs of Kom el-Shuqafa, which I shall discuss in detail, as the Centre for Alexandrian Studies (Centre d'Etudes Alexandrines: CEA) has been working on them. I shall also be mentioning the houses of the Alexandrians, their necropoleis and certain important buildings such as the Pharos lighthouse or the Caesareum in connection with the excavations I have been able to undertake in the course of the last ten years.

For everything else – be it literary sources or archaeological sites which have been reported on elsewhere – the reader is advised to refer to existing works on the capital of the Ptolemies. Undoubtedly the best of these is still P. M. Fraser's *Ptolemaic Alexandria* (1972), supplemented by Christoph Haas' *Alexandria in Late Antiquity* (1997).

This tomb was discovered in the east of the city by Adriani, in Tigranes Pasha Street (now Port Said Street). Its wall-paintings, which were removed to save them from the developers, are now in the garden of the archaeological site of the Kom el-Shuqafa catacombs. This naive painting dates from the end of the first century AD. On the corridor wall can be seen a pharaoh and, above him, the Apis bull. In the chapel, above one of the three sarcophagi in the room, Osiris is shown being mummified. The other scenes represent the resurrection and the adoration of Osiris. The ceiling is in Greek style: a Medusa head surrounded by felines chasing cervids.

BELOW: In one of the Anfushi tombs, a chapel is decorated with alternating palm trees and olive trees (or possibly sycomore-fig trees).

RIGHT: A wholly pharaonic scene is painted on the stairwell of another of the Anfushi tombs (second century BC).

figures as Botti, Breccia, Adriani, Rowe and Rodziewicz, most of the monuments mentioned in the ancient sources are for us still only names without any trace of physical remains. It is as if these buildings were suspended in the air above the map, waiting for us to find a clue that would enable them to land.

Moreover, the physical conditions have not always made the archaeologists' work easy. The ancient strata lie deeply buried, often below the water-table, the level of which has risen as a result of the subsidence that has profoundly affected the area. One frequently has to dig down ten metres (32 ft) or more to reach the installations of Alexandria's first citizens.

In view of these gaps in our knowledge, I felt that I could present this book neither as a guide to the ancient city nor as a historical survey based on the ancient texts: many such works have been written already. While it is true that it has been possible to save a certain number of sites, in spite of the obstacles mentioned above, it seemed to me preferable to illustrate the future hopes of Alexandrian archaeology from my own experience.

I shall mention only for the record the remains visible today. A good

expedition in the 1890s. Naturally, his colleagues got the message, and the exploration of the ancient city was directed by local archaeologists with limited means and by civil servants directly answerable to the hierarchic local administration. In spite of their enthusiasm, they must often have found themselves torn between their loyalty to the administration and their respect for the objects it was their duty to save. I must confess I would have found such constraints impossibly frustrating.

This is why the part of the ancient city we know best is the ancient cemeteries, which lay outside the walls and which were discovered as the result of construction projects only after the city centre had become too built-up to permit effective intervention by the Archaeological Service, which came into existence in the 1890s, around fifty years after the development of the modern city had started to gain momentum.

Over the past century, the increase in our knowledge of Alexandrian archaeology has been only modest. Despite the efforts of such outstanding

Mustafa Kamal: the tomb next door to the preceding one. We are in the open-air atrium: in the centre is an altar for the sacrifices performed in honour of the dead; in the background, doorways guarded by three pairs of little sphinxes lead into the burial chambers. Between the Doric columns, a painted panel shows a Macedonian horseman in three-quarter view in a scene that is clearly the work of a talented artist.

Plan of the sites excavated by the Centre for Alexandrian Studies (CEA) since 1992.

the royal palaces. These original works of the second century BC give an impression of the virtuosity of the Alexandrian mosaic-makers, bearing out the praises bestowed upon them by such ancient authors as Pliny the Elder.

In 1992 the authorities invited the Centre for Alexandrian Studies to undertake some joint excavations on various sites under threat in the city. Thanks to financial help from the French Foreign Ministry, the National Research Centre (CNRS), the French School at Athens and the French Institute of Oriental Archaeology (IFAO) in Cairo, the Centre has conducted about ten rescue digs in three different areas: the inhabited area of the city centre, two underwater zones outside the Eastern Harbour, and also, most recently, the western necropolis (Gabbari).[6]

In contrast to the systematic excavations undertaken by the Polish mission at Kom el-Dikka on a site acquired specifically for archaeological purposes, the rescue digs form a discipline of their own, with advantages but also numerous constraints. The most trying of these are the limited periods of grace granted to the archaeologists, who are obliged to return the excavated plot to its owner after a short space of time – in most cases, only a few months. Moreover, they can hardly ever choose where to dig as they are dependent on the twists and turns of the developers' activities. In fact, such intensive restructuring of the city centre at least makes it possible to determine priorities. Accordingly, we have confined ourselves to the eastern area of the ancient quarter of the Caesareum and the western fringes of the Brucheion, not far from the place where Schliemann's abortive trial digs took place. One advantage is seeing a kind of jigsaw puzzle being fitted together bit by bit. Another is that the aim of a rescue dig is to investigate the archaeological strata down to the natural rock; in other words, to the first structures that the Alexandrians built upon it. It is by no means the aim of these investigations to hold back the development of the modern city: only in the case of an

Egypt's peace treaty with Israel changed the situation. Since President Sadat's visit to Jerusalem in 1977 and the liberalisation of the Egyptian economy, capital has been invested in property and developers in both Cairo and Alexandria lie in wait for the rare building plots which are still available, and above all for large uneconomical buildings. Since residential buildings are protected by strict social legislation, they fall back on cinemas, theatres, garages and warehouses. Such buildings are flimsy structures, with shallow foundations that have left the ancient foundations on which they are built intact,

thus preserving the substratum. Contrary to common belief, the urbanization of the nineteenth century has not eradicated the ancient city forever.

The problem has rapidly shown itself to be in many ways very similar to the one the nineteenth-century archaeologists had to contend with. It involves following the movements of building contractors, something which is not always easy. Like their counterparts the world over, the developers at Alexandria often try to evade irksome conservation orders. There are a great many development projects, and the Egyptian Archaeological Service tries to hold its ground on many fronts, but the bulldozers make more rapid progress than the archaeologists.

In 1993 the work on the foundations of the new Bibliotheca Alexandrina became a test case: in the sides of the trenches two magnificent Hellenistic floor mosaics in *opus vermiculatum* were uncovered in what was once the quarter of

Emergency rescue excavations at the Diana Theatre. On this site it has been possible to uncover, among other things, a large house of the Roman period (second century AD).

It was not until the 1960s that new discoveries were made in the city centre. The directors – all of them Egyptians from 1954 – were energetic, and the second of them, Henri Riad, uncovered some new tombs in the western necropolis, in particular one decorated with a water-wheel – one of the museum's prize exhibits – and a segment of the south colonnade of the Canopic Street.[4] Not far from there, about 100 metres to the south-west on the site of Kom el-Dikka, a Napoleonic fort had been destroyed; the plan was to build council flats there, but the bulldozers hit upon the upper rows

of a theatre. It was the first to be discovered in a city which, according to an ancient source, once had four hundred of them.

It was a sign of the times and of Egypt's choice of allies under President Nasser that the excavation was entrusted to a Polish mission, which for the past thirty-five years has been systematically exploring what has become the city's largest archaeological park. Besides the odeum, now completely cleared and restored, a Roman bath complex and a whole residential quarter dating from the Ptolemaic through to the medieval period have been uncovered and published. Part of the site is open to visitors while the excavators proceed.

In the early 1970s, German archaeological missions made a hesitant appearance on the scene in the necropoleis of Hadra and Gabbari,[5] but in spite of some successful discoveries followed by detailed publications, it seems unlikely that they will continue.

tions were conducted by the directors of this institution. Three Italian scholars held this post in succession: Giuseppe Botti (1892–1904), Evaristo Breccia (1904–32) and Achille Adriani (1932–40 and 1948–52) all brought vigour and dedication to the job. It was they who conducted practically all the excavations and investigations in the city and the surrounding area. Hogarth's prediction therefore seemed to have come true: research at Alexandria was destined for 'those who have a local interest in the site', not for foreign institutions.

The archaeological expedition of the German Ernst von Sieglin had arrived a few years before Hogarth and for more than a generation produced a series of remarkable discoveries and publications. We are indebted to it for a supplement to el-Falaki's map and for excavations in the catacombs of Kom el-Shuqafa and other tombs. The reports written at the time about these undertakings are still indispensable reference works for today's scholars. One should add Ferdinand Noack's exploratory excavations of the streets in the city centre and Hermann Thiersch's seminal book which, although it appeared almost a century ago, is still the basis of all research on the Pharos.

Besides these exemplary expeditions, which greatly increased our knowledge of the grid of the city's streets, its monumental buildings and necropoleis, one must not forget the tireless activity of the three Italian directors. Their unflagging energy, their continued struggle against the quarrymen and entrepreneurs, and the rapidity with which they published the results of their labours were truly astonishing. Certainly, the archaeological quality, both of the excavations themselves and of the reports, improved over the decades, and if Adriani is acknowledged to have been more competent than Botti, it is in part because of his more exacting scientific standards. There were few investigations in the city centre, since the area between the railway station and the tramway terminal had become densely built up from 1870–80 onwards, but the necropoleis – el-Shuqafa, Shatby, Anfushi, Hadra, Mustafa Kamal – gave up their secrets one after the other. Thus, while the museum filled up, it must be admitted that the discoveries were made above all in the outlying quarters, in the ancient cemeteries situated outside the Ptolemaic city walls.

During the Second World War, Adriani was interned in a concentration camp, like all the Italians and Germans resident in Egypt. The new director, Alan Rowe, a Briton, was an experienced archaeologist and made some lucky finds. He tackled the flattened ruins of the sanctuary of Sarapis and dug up the bilingual foundation tablets which are now among the choicest exhibits in the museum. He also, like Botti and von Sieglin, explored the catacombs of Kom el-Shuqafa and excavated the third level there, uncovering a tomb that had not been robbed.

OPPOSITE PAGE: The Roman odeum at Kom el-Dikka in its present state. This small covered theatre dates from the fourth century AD.

ing apart the ancient necropoleis, and to try to save the occasional wall-painting or sculpture. The buildings erected during the years 1850–1900 consolidated the city, giving it the appearance which the centre still has today.

From Hogarth's time archaeological research in Alexandria was entirely in the hands of the local authorities. They had a certain number of documents to help them – first of all, the maps and plans which the scholars of the French expedition to Egypt published in the *Description de l'Egypte*. One of these represents Alexandria as it appeared in 1798–1801; the other, on a smaller scale, the town and its territory. An inventory of ancient monuments was illustrated with a dozen engraved plates. The authors of these works, Alexandre Saint-Genis and Gratien Le Père, worked with such quality and precision that their work superseded all the descriptions written by travellers of the preceding centuries.

It was another fifty years or more before the next significant advance came, with the work of Mahmud el-Falaki, astronomer (*falaki* in Arabic but he was in fact an engineer, trained in Paris as a cartographer) to the Ottoman viceroy the Khedive Ismaïl. It is well known that Napoleon III took it on himself to write a biography of Caesar. To help him draft his chapter on the Alexandrian war, he turned to his friend Khedive Ismaïl with the request for a plan of the ancient city. Mahmud el-Falaki was thus given the means to draw up a plan of the city and was able to conduct more than 200 exploratory digs in the built-up area, which at that time hardly extended beyond the peninsula.[2] The French emperor, however, completed only the first volumes – not including the one on Alexandria – before his defeat at Sedan in 1870. Consequently, Mahmud el-Falaki decided to publish his plan in Copenhagen in 1872, six years after he had completed it. It is an outstanding work, reflecting the considerable resources employed in its production, rendered even more effective by the support of the Khedive and the solid training of its maker. Almost a century and a half after its publication it is still used as a reference work by archaeologists working at Alexandria.[3]

The second half of the nineteenth century saw other enterprises, some more valuable than others. Apart from the brief and fruitless involvement of Hogarth and Schliemann, the fate of archaeological research at Alexandria was linked to the presence of enlightened amateurs such as Tassos Neroutzos, who during the 1870s visited building sites and recorded the alignment of walls and above all Greek inscriptions, which his classical education enabled him to publish without delay in international scholarly journals.

The foundation in 1892 of the Graeco-Roman Museum marked a turning point. During the following decades excavations and topographical investiga-

A couple from the pharaonic period in pink Aswan granite, found during Botti's excavations in Alexandria at the end of the nineteenth century.

journal in which he declared that 'no foreign [archaeological] society which can find almost virgin sites, could be invited to search in Alexandria for obscure Graeco-Roman ruins … or bare topographical indications.'[1]

The final blow was administered by the great Heinrich Schliemann himself. The discoverer of Troy and Mycenae disembarked at Alexandria with the avowed aim of finding the tomb of Alexander, no less. He must have become disillusioned, initially because the excavation permits took a long time to come through (he wanted to dig beside the Nabi-Danyal Mosque).

An engraving made in 1681 by the Dutch traveller Cornelius Le Bruyn. The two columns were part of the Canopic Street. In the background on the left is the Tower of the Romans, and behind it in the distance the Eastern Harbour and Fort Qait Bey.

While he was waiting, he opened up some exploratory trenches near Ramleh station (not far from the place where we believe the Caesareum stood) and in his turn uncovered only late Roman layers. Disgusted, he left Alexandria at once to go on a leisure cruise on the Nile.

Finally, the third reason why attempts to explore the remains of Alexandria came to nothing is associated with the rapid expansion of the city from the mid-nineteenth century onwards. The Europeans and Levantines who, encouraged by the viceroy Mohammed Ali, came looking for a better future in this new, unexploited El Dorado, did not allow cultural concerns or scruples to hold them up. Thanks to them an entire well-preserved Roman camp in the eastern quarter of the city disappeared, as did the city walls, the blocks of which were used to build the settlers' city. The local archaeological authorities had no choice other than to follow in the wake of the quarrymen, who were busy tear-

CARTE
DE L'ANTIQUE ALEXANDRIE
ET DE SES FAUBOURGS
Dressée
sur les ordres de S.A. le Vice-Roi d'Egypte
à l'aide de fouilles, nivellements et autres recherches
par MAHMOUD-BEY, Astronome de Son Altesse
Fait en 1866

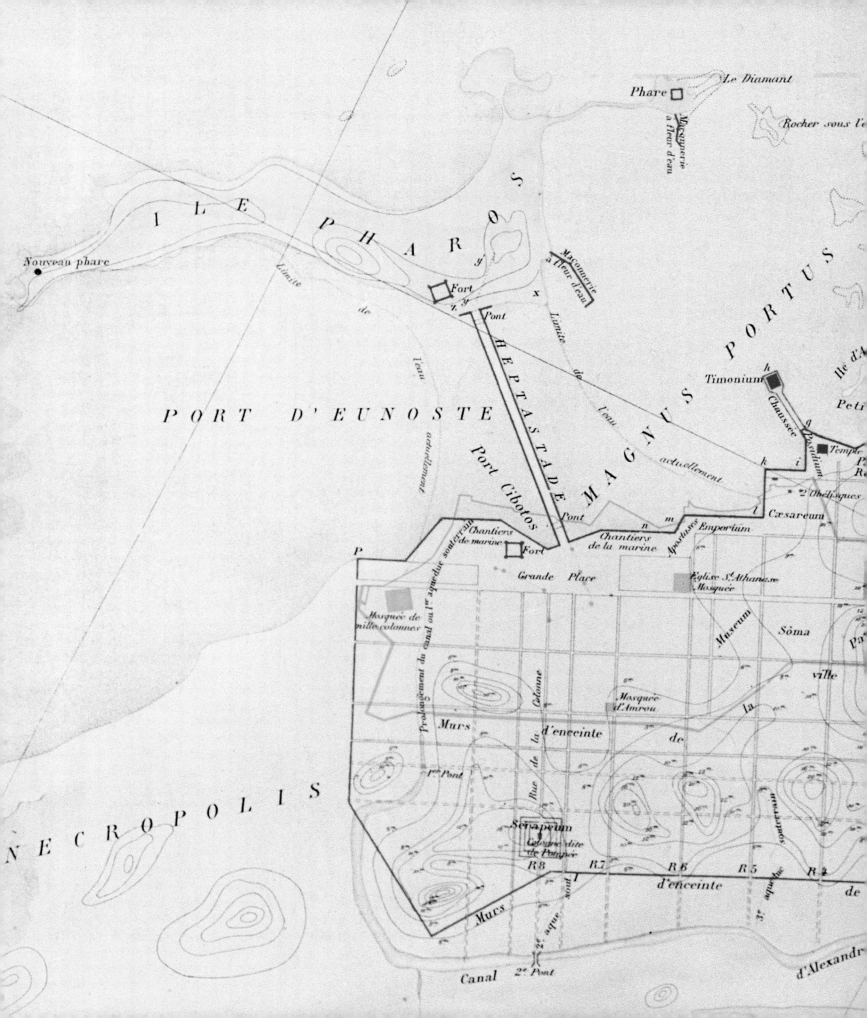

famous buildings of antiquity, of the palace of the Ptolemies, and even more so of the tomb of Alexander the Great. One can see why the archaeologists who work at Alexandria find themselves in a strange situation: they have more information about most of the little Greek towns of the Mediterranean world than about the greatest of the Hellenistic cities, the only one able to compete with Rome in terms of wealth, size, cultural prestige and population. There are several reasons for this lack of information.

It was not Alexandria that attracted the scholars who came to Egypt in the nineteenth century. They disembarked there in order to reach Cairo quickly, from where they would set out to discover the temples of Upper Egypt. A good number of these temples (Edfu, Dendera, Kom Ombo, Philae and others) were built by Alexander's successors and attest to the vitality of the three centuries of Greek rule in the land of the pharaohs (331–30 BC). How could the meagre remains of the Ptolemies' capital be a match for these imposing, almost perfectly preserved monuments? The valley of the Nile soon became the preserve of Egyptologists, who developed their discipline by deciphering the miles of inscriptions which cover the walls of the temples and the innumerable objects unearthed. Admittedly, the Graeco-Roman period did receive a certain amount of attention, as the hunt for papyri led to excavations in the little towns around the edges of the Fayum. This kind of document, however, does not survive in the climate of Alexandria, which is a great pity, because otherwise people would have taken a quite different interest in the archaeology of the city, and our knowledge of it would have been transformed.

The second half of the nineteenth century saw the foundation of the great Archaeological Institutes at Athens, Rome and Cairo. The French School at Athens led the way in 1846, soon followed by the German Archaeological Institute, the British School and others (today there are seventeen altogether). They organized major expeditions throughout Greece and the Eastern Mediterranean, sharing out the important sites: the French got Delphi and Delos, the Germans Olympia, the British Knossos, and so on.

Scholars visited Turkey and the Levant, but Alexandria hardly figured in their itineraries. It was only in 1894 (twenty years after excavations were begun on Delos) that the British School at Athens assigned to one of its researchers, D.G. Hogarth, the task of evaluating Alexandria's archaeological potential. His investigation, however, was a short-lived affair: he did indeed start an excavation at Kom-el-Dikka (near the Roman odeum which was uncovered subsequently), but after digging through several metres of rubble he had only just reached the levels of the late Roman period. Having stayed for scarcely two months, he published a report in a widely read scholarly

OVERLEAF: Plan of ancient Alexandria drawn up by Mahmud el-Falaki. Dated 1866, it shows the results of 200 trial excavations. The street grid and the walls can be clearly seen. In spite of the criticisms levelled at it in the later nineteenth century, this plan is still used by archaeologists today.

ARCHAEOLOGICAL RESEARCH IN ALEXANDRIA is now more than a hundred years old: in 1992 the Graeco-Roman Museum and the local Archaeological Society celebrated their centenary. The number of excavations and trial digs runs into the hundreds and the storerooms of the museum are overflowing with a rich harvest of finds.

Even so, despite the considerable efforts of several generations of archaeologists, the results are generally (and wrongly, as this book sets out to show)

Until the eighteenth century, town plans of Alexandria tended to be fanciful panoramas that offered little information about its topography. It is usually possible to identify the canal that comes from the Nile, its tributaries bringing water into the city, the massive Tulunid city walls, the Eastern Harbour and, shown here on the right, the Kibotos, or artificial harbour mentioned by Strabo. In front of the harbour entrance Fort Qait Bey can be seen on the right, and the Pharillon ('little lighthouse') on the left.

regarded as meagre. Forget Athens and Rome: here there are no temples still standing, no Parthenon, no Colosseum, no ancient monuments which form a visible part of the urban landscape; practically no trace of the capital of the Ptolemies can be seen above ground. Only Pompey's Pillar remains upright, unaffected by all the earthquakes that Alexandria has suffered through the ages. It is one of the paradoxes of history that this column, which was erected in honour of the Emperor Diocletian at the end of the third century AD, has survived unscathed. It dominates the foundations of the great temple of Sarapis, of which nothing else survives. The ancient writers, however, tell us that this sanctuary was one of the jewels of the ancient world; so too was the Caesareum, the splendours of which are described by Philo. It, too, has completely disappeared, and all one can do is to form some idea of its location.

The same is true of the Library and the Mouseion, both among the most

CHAPTER ONE

A century of archaeological research

OPPOSITE: Early
excavations. In this
picture taken at the
end of the
nineteenth century
Giuseppe Botti, the
founder of the
Graeco-Roman
Museum (1892),
is inspecting the
remains of an Ionic
peristyle courtyard in
a large tomb in the
Karmuz quarter, not
far from Pompey's
Pillar.

This engraving by
Luigi Meyer (1802) is
entitled 'The Baths of
Cleopatra'. In reality,
it represents the
façade of a tomb
situated on the shore
of the present
Western Harbour,
in the necropolis.

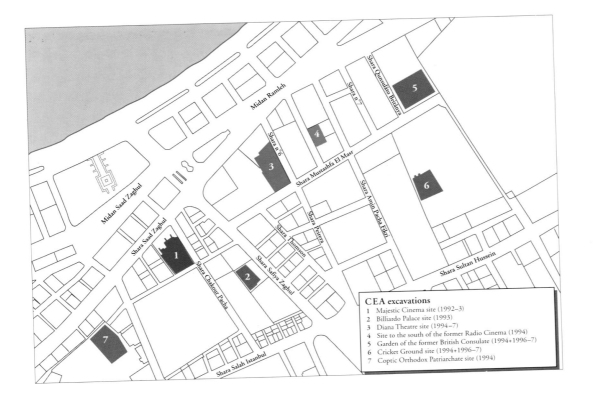

Detail of the preceding plan: in the ancient quarter of Brucheion, south-east of the royal palaces.

CEA excavations

1 Majestic Cinema site (1992–3)
2 Billiardo Palace site (1993)
3 Diana Theatre site (1994–7)
4 Site to the south of the former Radio Cinema (1994)
5 Garden of the former British Consulate (1994+1996–7)
6 Cricket Ground site (1994+1996–7)
7 Coptic Orthodox Patriarchate site (1994)

exceptional discovery would the expropriation of the plots concerned be considered, something which has not happened so far.

The six years of emergency excavations carried out by the CEA have been fruitful. They have enabled us, in several places, to reconstruct the stratigraphic sequence through all the phases of occupation from the Mamluk period (1250–1517) right back to the first generations of settlers. Ten metres of stratigraphy have allowed us to uncover 2,300 years of history.

The level of occupation of the recent centuries was slight.[7] The Ottomans chose to install themselves on the spit which had formed on either side of the Heptastadion (the causeway that linked the island of Pharos with the mainland). What is now the quarter around Ramleh station, on which our efforts are focused, was still just a belt of gardens: one finds coins, clay pipes and pottery there, but no buildings. The earliest phases of the Islamic period, the Fatimid and the Mamluk, are represented by a rich assortment of finds, including glazed pottery from all over the Mediterranean, from Ifriqiya and Andalusia to Syria, Iraq, Persia and China (with numerous pieces of celadon ware) – which bears witness to the wealth of Alexandria right up to the end of the fourteenth century, a period when the city fell into a decline from which the ports of Rosetta and Damietta, which were better protected from Christian raids, profited.

CHAPTER TWO

The site of Alexandria

OPPOSITE: The rectangular area of the Latin cemeteries by the intersection of the streets *R1* and *L1*, the two principal thoroughfares of the ancient city. It is thought that Alexander the Great's tomb was situated in the royal necropolis north-east of this crossroads. The University of Alexandria has recently started excavating there.

Detail of a watercolour by J.-C. Golvin showing the eastern end of the island of Pharos, with the Lighthouse and the Heptastadion, the causeway that connected the island with the mainland.

Map of Egypt in the Ptolemaic period. Alexandria, Naucratis and Ptolemais were the only Greek cities, with a citizen body organized in the traditional Greek way.

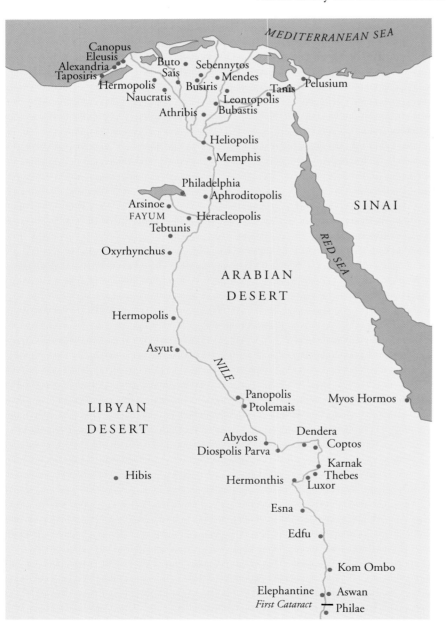

IN JANUARY 331 BC Alexander the Great left Memphis, which he had just subjugated, taking *de facto* control of the whole of Egypt. On his way to the Mediterranean coast he skirted the eastern edge of the Delta and decided to make a halt thirty kilometres (18 miles) further on, at a point on the coast between Lake Mariut and the sea. Off this narrow strip of coast, a good kilometre from the shore, lay the little island of Pharos, which was already familiar to Greek travellers.

What were the reasons that prompted Alexander to occupy this site, which many modern historians regard as a difficult one geographically and a poor choice? The area had neither an important past nor an abundant supply of good water to recommend it. But was Alexander deliberately ignoring the geographical problems, and how did this major handicap become an asset for the development of what was to become the great 'megalopolis' of the Hellenistic world and antiquity's liveliest city?

The state of mind he found himself in when he arrived at this place opposite Pharos makes it easier to understand the unexpected and paradoxical nature of his decision. To begin with, he had just conquered the Persians on his way through Asia Minor, inflicting upon them defeat after defeat, amassing a considerable amount of booty and making himself master of territories of a vastness beyond the wildest dreams of any Greek commander before him. Then, after a long siege, he had succeeded, despite enormous difficulties, in taking the city of Tyre, a fortress on an island joined to the mainland by an isthmus. Finally, having had little difficulty in getting rid of the last of the satraps who governed Egypt for the Great King of Persia, he had seized the valley of the Nile. The size and wealth of Memphis must have impressed him.

Egypt had fascinated the Greeks for centuries. Now, in the second half of the fourth century BC, it seemed to them, a people used to seafaring and commerce, to be a world of its own, closed and introspective. Although recent archaeological discoveries have shown that Ramses II's foundation of a new capital, Pi-Ramses, on the Pelusiac branch of the Nile, had opened Egypt up to the outside world on the north, in Alexander's time this town was no more than the ruins of a bygone age, and it was towards the old capital, Memphis, that he headed. Even if one believes that the mentality of the Egyptians had changed during the last dynasties of the pharaohs, one can still imagine that the Greeks must have felt this was a land that had withdrawn into itself: it was interested only in its valley, and regarded the deserts and the seas as frontiers and foreign parts. Even a port like Naucratis, which had been made over to merchants from Ionia in the seventh century BC, was not on the sea but seventy kilometres (45 miles) inland up the Delta. There was nothing on the coast apart from this obscure fishing village, 'Rhakotis', about which we have no information.

The demotic scholar Michel Chauveau explained recently that the Egyptians gave this name, Rhakotis (Ra-qed in Egyptian) – that is, 'building site' – to the newly founded city and that subsequently they consistently refused to call Alexander's capital by its Greek name.[13] This suggests that when he arrived here the only inhabitants of the area must have been a few fishermen and perhaps also a garrison stationed there to guard the approaches to the Delta. The Greek authors who wrote about the city and its history must have been misled by their ignorance of the Egyptian language into thinking that Rhakotis was a pre-existing native settlement, and modern historians have followed them, with the result that they have not explained the existence of pharaonic elements in the city correctly. We shall see this later on when we come to the excavation of the Pharos.

THE INSTINCT OF A GREEK confronted with a newly conquered country was to open it up, to find a way of getting it out of its shell, to establish communications between this new dominion and the outside world, primarily of course with the Mediterranean – the 'frog pond', as Plato called it. It was typically Greek behaviour to look for a site facing north in order to promote sea-going traffic with the rest of the Greek world.

But which was the right place to choose? Not a site in the Delta, which flooded when the Nile rose. The Greek writers, in particular Herodotus (whom Alexander had read under the supervision of his teacher Aristotle),

OVERLEAF: View from a helicopter of the eastern part of the Ottoman town, which grew up from 1517 onwards on land around the ancient Heptastadion. In the foreground is the Abu el-Abbas el-Morsi Mosque, consecrated to one of the most venerated Muslim saints of Alexandria. Behind it is the basin of the Eastern Harbour and Cape Lochias (now the Silsila promontory), which encloses the harbour on the east.

A site overlooking the 'frog pond'

Watercolour by J.-C. Golvin showing Alexandria's situation in relation to the western part of the Nile Delta. Lake Mariut and Lake Edku are separated by the Canopic branch of the Nile, now no longer in existence. Further to the left in the far distance one can just make out Sais and Naucratis, the Greek city founded by merchants in the seventh century BC.

related how in summer only the villages remained above water, forming so many islands in a temporary sea and constituting a veritable trap (as several invaders had found out during the course of history). Alexander the Great preferred good, solid, rocky ground that did not give way under one's feet or disappear beneath the waters during the Nile flood.

The importance of the island of Pharos

A SHORT DISTANCE from the marshes and canals of the Delta there was such a site: Rhakotis had the further advantage of lying opposite an island. It is well known that the Greeks had a special liking for offshore islands, especially when their control of the mainland was poor and the local population hostile. This had been one of the guiding principles of Greek colonization since the Archaic period: take the island and make it a safe base before trying to take the mainland. This traditional approach is well illustrated by the adventures of the Greeks in the eighth century BC on the little island of Pithecussa off Naples.

Similarly, in Egypt the site of Mersa Matruh, about 300 kilometres (185 miles) west of the future Alexandria, had served for a long time as a port of entry for Greeks making a pilgrimage to the oasis of Siwa. The city which they founded there, Ammonia or, in the Roman period, Paraetonium, offered the same advantage: Bates Island, a short swim from the coast, had served them as a trading post since the Mycenaean period, as has been shown by the excavations carried out there by an American team a few years ago.

The island of Pharos itself was by no means unknown to the Greeks, since Homer set an episode of the *Odyssey* there (4.351–586). The story of the dream of Alexander, who according to authors such as Pseudo-Callisthenes and Plutarch chose this site following the blind poet's directions, is not absurd: after all the *Iliad* and the *Odyssey* were his favourite bedtime reading.

The foundation in the literal sense of the word was carried out with the help of the architect Dinocrates of Rhodes following a comprehensive plan: first came the walls, then the street grid and the harbours, and last but not least a highly efficient fresh-water supply.

OPPOSITE PAGE: Head of Alexander the Great in Aswan pink granite. The use of this stone shows that it was carved in Egypt, probably at the end of the Hellenistic period. Graeco-Roman Museum, Alexandria.

CHAPTER THREE

City walls,
houses and streets

OPPOSITE: Medusa mosaic. This medallion graced the dining-room floor of a house of the Roman period (second century AD) uncovered in the excavation on the site of the former Diana Theatre.

Detail from an engraving in the *Description de l'Egypte*, showing the city walls.

The foundation legend

RIGHT FROM THE BEGINNING of the project, the planners had intended Alexandria to be of dimensions hitherto unknown among Greek cities. The foundation legend illustrates this: Alexander presided in person at the marking out of the city limits, about which Strabo says, 'Writers record, as a sign of the good fortune that has since attended the city, an incident which occurred at the time of tracing the lines of the foundation: when the architects were marking the lines of the enclosure with chalk [lit. 'white earth'] the supply of chalk gave out; and when the king arrived, his stewards furnished a part of the barley-meal which had been prepared for the workmen, and by means of this the streets also, to a larger number than before, were laid out. This occurrence, then, they are said to have interpreted as a good omen.'[14]

In his *Life of Alexander* Plutarch gives us more details about the end of this story and the Macedonian king's reaction: '… but suddenly birds from the river and the lagoon, infinite in number and of every sort and size, set-

Engraving by L.F. Cassas (1784), looking east along the Canopic Street by the Attarine Mosque.

OPPOSITE PAGE: Watercolour by J.-C. Golvin showing the Canopic Street looking west from its intersection with the main north-south axis (crossing of *R1* and *L1*).

tled down upon the place like clouds and devoured every particle of the barley-meal, so that even Alexander was greatly disturbed at the omen. However the seers exhorted him to be of good cheer, since the city here founded by him would have most abundant and helpful resources and be a nursing mother for men of every nation'.[15]

The city walls

THE CITY CAME INTO EXISTENCE once its limits had been marked out and building work had started on the walls that enclosed it. This circuit, which determined the size of its surface area, measured, according to various ancient writers, a good fifteen kilometres (9 miles), which makes it the biggest

The Crétin Fort, named after an officer in the Corps of Engineers of Napoleon's army, abuts the Tulunid city wall.

ancient urban enclosure after Athens and Syracuse. But it must be stressed that the walls of Athens included its port, the Piraeus, while those of Syracuse (as elsewhere in Sicily) encompassed arable and pasture land to enable the citizens to survive sieges. One has only to compare the plans of the built-up areas of these different urban conglomerations to realize that the new city was of an enormous size, comparable in this respect only with Rome, and that it was inevitable that they would one day become rivals in a struggle to the death during which the fate of the world would hang in the balance.

These ramparts proved effective enough to withstand several attackers. During the Ptolemaic period, enemy armies rarely reached the city: Antiochus of Syria besieged it in 170 BC, but had to give up before the strength of its defences. As we have seen, however, they did give way on several occasions during the Roman period: in AD 269 to Queen Zenobia of Palmyra, and in the following year to Aurelian when he retook the city. As for Diocletian, who came to Egypt in 297 to get rid of a usurper, it took him a month to gain control of the city. Later on, at the beginning of the seventh century, the Sasanians managed to take it by storm. It was finally to fall for good by treason in 640, when, in defiance of Byzantium, a section of the population opened the gates to the troops of the Arab general Amr.

Tracing the exact course of the ancient walls is no easy task. In fact, we do

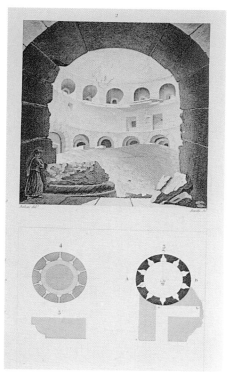

not even know how many of them we are dealing with: probably a Hellenistic wall which was enlarged in the Roman period and supplemented by a second, medieval, one begun, if not built, by Sultan Ahmed Ibn Tulun in the ninth century. This last does not pose an insoluble problem, in so far as it is often mentioned in the accounts of Arab and European travellers, who enlarge with admiration on the height of its walls, the number of its towers and the fittings of its gates.

Benoît de Maillet, for instance, who was French Consul General at Alexandria from 1692 onwards, wrote after his return to France: 'This new circuit is a double one: first an outer wall bars the approaches, and, at about thirty paces from it, a second wall faces inwards onto the city. Between these two walls, by means of passageways or arcades cut in the towers along the walls at ground level, the troops whose duty it was to guard the city were able to make their rounds protected by the double wall from attacks either from without or within. These towers, of which even the smallest is a kind of fortress, project considerably both on the outside and on the inside. Thus they will easily hold four or five hundred men, so that an army of fifty thousand men could be accommodated in them without being a burden on the inhabitants. The towers are vaulted throughout and each of them has more than a hundred rooms. Moreover, I am pretty well convinced by those

ABOVE LEFT: Inside the massive city walls at the east end of the Canopic Street. The medieval masonry consists of small stones and rubble infill.

ABOVE RIGHT: The Tower of the Romans, part of the ancient city walls altered and restored in the ninth century by Ibn Tulun. This tower stood on the shore of the Eastern Harbour, a few metres to the east of Cleopatra's Needles. It was demolished at the beginning of the twentieth century.

people who believe that these extraordinarily high towers were built in two stages. One can still distinguish today the work of the prince who had them made higher than they had been before by the care he took to have them roughcast. Further, in the first ditch at the side of each tower there are posterns through which the troops could make sorties. It cannot be denied that this city was very strongly fortified in those days.'

The Englishman Richard Pococke, who visited Alexandria in 1737, was also full of admiration: 'The first thing I did at Alexandria was to pace round the walls, and take the bearings; which I did with so much caution, that I thought I could only have been observed by the Janizary that attended me; notwithstanding it was soon publickly reported about the town that I had measured the city walls by palms. [...] The outer walls round the old city are very beautifully built of hewn stone, and seem to be antient; all the arches being true, and the workmanship very good: They are defended by semicircular towers, twenty feet diameter, and about one hundred and thirty feet apart; [...] The inner walls of the old city, which seem to be of the middle ages, are much stronger and higher than the others, and defended by large high towers. There are particularly two very large well-built towers to the north-west, towards the new city on the strand.'

Consul Maillet, like other travellers, observed that this double city wall was constructed of an assortment of building materials, of stones purloined from various ancient monuments: 'Moreover, the walls of this new Alexandria and the hundred towers which flank them are built of thousands of pieces of marble and broken columns interspersed with stones, which proves conclusively that this city has been built on the ruins of the ancient one, and that its walls do not date from Antiquity as such.'

In our excavations we have found traces of this salvaging of ancient blocks by the Tulunid builders. In the excavation of the former Diana Theatre, for instance, we uncovered deep trenches: ancient walls had been pulled down and their blocks reused to build the rampart which runs close to this spot. A whole section of the face of this medieval wall has recently been cleared by Mohammed Abdel Aziz, whose work has shown that it was nine metres (29½ ft) high. It had been repaired in 1826 by Galice Bey, the French general employed by Mohammed Ali. After this period, however, it proved to have outlived its usefulness and even became an obstacle to the expansion of the city. Accordingly, it was demolished at the end of the nineteenth century. A few sections of it still exist, in the Shallalat Gardens, for instance, at the stadium or again, to the west of the city, at the Green Gate.

Fragment of Attic pottery, predating the foundation of the city (around 375 BC). Found in the excavations at the former garden of the British Consulate.

ABOVE: The outer face of the city wall in the Shallalat Gardens. This is the only place in the city where a section of the Hellenistic wall has survived. It is built of courses of large blocks; the bosses for lifting are still clearly visible on some of them.

LEFT: One of the Tulunid towers abutting the wall of the Graeco-Roman period.

Thanks to various plans, with sections of the towers, especially those in *Description de l'Egypte*, we possess reliable and relatively precise document-ation of these ramparts, which are now mostly no longer in existence.

The question of the ancient city wall, on the other hand, is far less straightforward. Next to nothing is left of it today: only one last vestige remains in the Shallalat Gardens. The last but one was destroyed at the beginning of the twentieth century: it belonged to the seaward face of the wall and comprised a round tower, traditionally known as the Tower of the Romans. This name was inappropriate, for the engravings, plans and sec-tions as well as the photographs of it show a construction of large, isodomic blocks without mortar, in the Hellenistic style. The tower in the Shallalat Gardens is similarly built in imposing, regular courses. Yvon Garlan, who has recently resumed the study of the walls of Alexandria, has pointed out that both the Roman Tower and that of Shallalat are built of shelly lime-stone, which is not normally used in the buildings of Alexandria.

As for the function of the Shallalat tower, this involves the wider problem of the eastern limits of the city. Did the tower, which is situated south of Cape Lochias, form part of the circuit of the walls, and did the oldest cemeteries, like Shatby, where the first generations of Alexandrians were buried, lie beyond that? In his plan of 1866 and his commentary of 1872, Mahmud el-Falaki records a second wall 2,300 metres (about 2,500 yds) east of the Shallalat Gate: could it be a Roman fortification which would have encompassed the Hellenis-tic cemeteries? Only excavations can provide an answer to this problem.

For the rest of the circuit, the sea forms a natural barrier in the north, while on the south and west sides the freshwater canal serves the same purpose. As the walls have not been the object of any recent excavations, I can only refer to the results obtained by Mahmud el-Falaki on the basis of his investigations.

As far as the number of the towers and gates is concerned, our ignorance remains almost total. The main east–west artery ended in the east at the Canopic Gate. Is this the Greek gate or its Roman extension, further still to the east, which, from the second century AD on, would come to be known as the Gate of the Sun? At the other end of the street, five kilometres (3 miles) to the west, lies its counterpart, the Gate of the Moon, which leads to the necropolis. This too was built in the Roman period – under Hadrian or Antoninus Pius.

The streets

ACCORDING TO THE ANCIENT WRITERS, the street grid was part of the original plan. Diodorus Siculus attributes it to the king, that is to Alexander himself: 'It was conveniently situated near the harbour of Pharos, and by selecting the right angle of the streets, Alexander made the city

OPPOSITE PAGE: This segment of the Tulunid city wall was discovered during work on a road tunnel and uncovered by Mohammed Abdel Aziz, Director General of Islamic Antiquities in the Western Delta, who was able to reconstruct it not far from the original find spot. It is seen here at its full height (over 9 m; 29 ft): these walls must certainly have been impressive.

OVERLEAF: Watercolour by J.-C. Golvin, showing Alexandria seen from the south, from Lake Mariut. In the foreground is the artist's impression of the harbours on the lake, of which no physical traces have survived. Strabo says that they were more important than the maritime harbours.

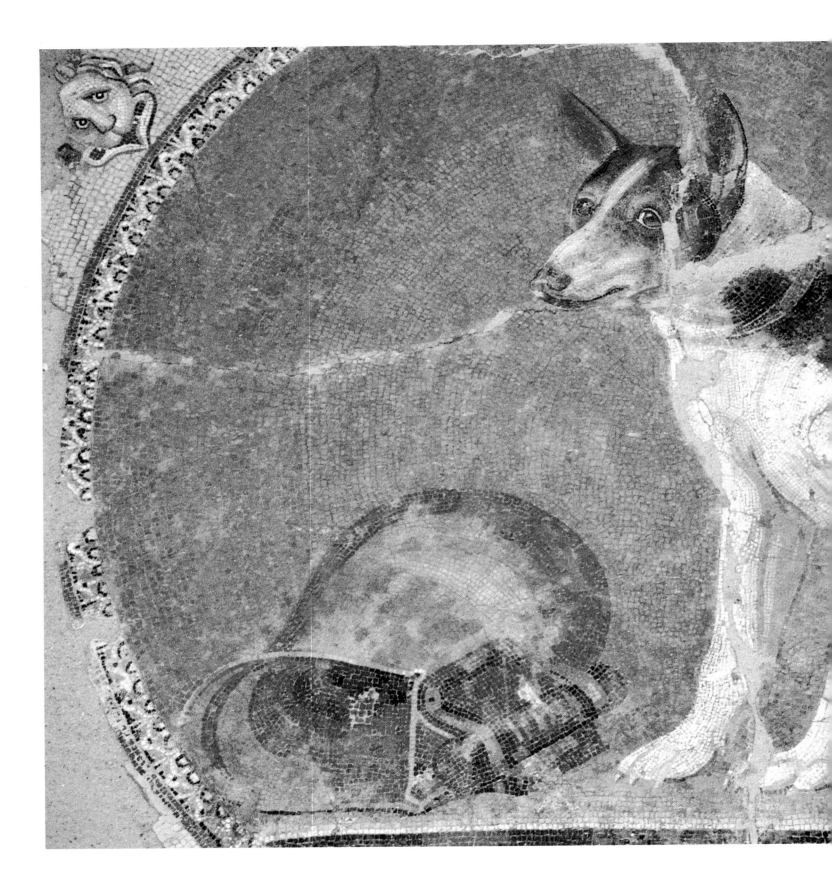

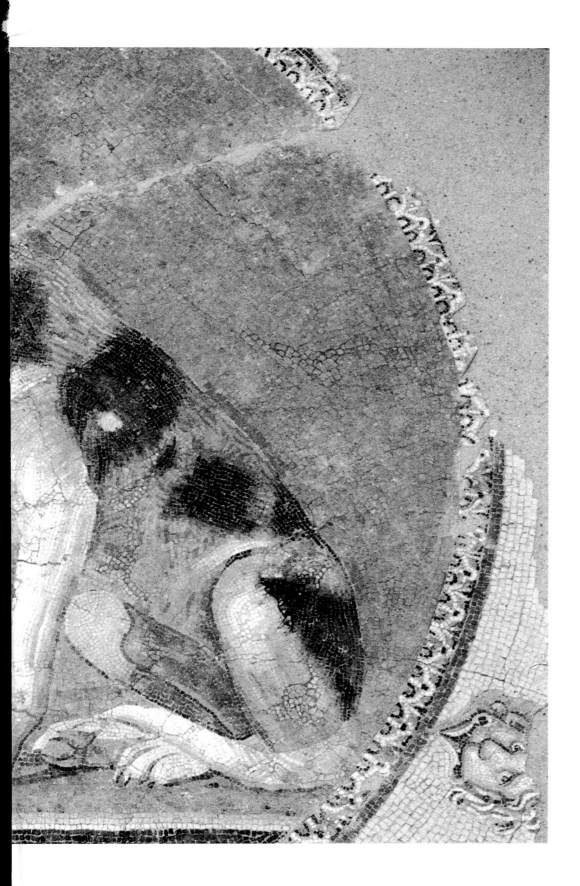

Mosaic of a dog found in the Egyptian Archaeological Service's excavation on the site of the future Bibliotheca Alexandrina. This is the central medallion, the *emblema,* depicting a domesticated dog (shown by the red collar). He is sitting, with his tail curled round his back legs, beside a bronze *askos*. Is this the moral of a fable? The ancient fabulists, Aesop in particular, often gave dogs a role in their stories, but none of them seems to be about a dog with a spilt jug. The mosaic is in *opus vermiculatum*, made of tiny tesserae only a few millimetres across, and is an original work of the second century BC.

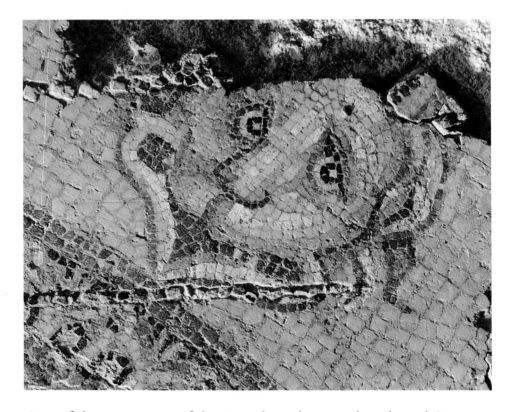

Detail of the border round the
Dog Mosaic with one of the six
lion-headed protomes.

tions of the greater part of the city, Alexander gave them letters' (or numbers, according to Greek usage). The second district might correspond to
the palace quarter (as is suggested by a lapidary inscription), the fourth to
the Jewish quarter. Initially, at least, these quarters will have made possible
the registration of the citizens in the city registers following the classical
system of tribes and demes.

Recent archaeological discoveries show that the urban infrastructure
could vary from quarter to quarter. I take as examples two excavations carried out in recent years, one of the Ptolemaic, one of the Roman period. In
the rescue dig at the former British Consulate in the western part of the
Brucheion quarter (i.e. to the south-west of the royal palaces), a house of
the first half of the third century BC has been found. It contains numerous
rooms, including a sumptuous dining-room or *triclinium* with an interesting
pebble mosaic floor in the Macedonian tradition (a reminder that a good
many of the first Alexandrians were from Macedonia). The house is very
large and richly decorated, but we cannot tell from the excavations whether
it had an upper storey.

Two hundred metres (220 yds) to the west of this site, the excavations at
the former Diana Theatre have uncovered a large house of the second century AD with a dozen floor mosaics, including a dining-room floor with a

LEFT: Emergency excavations in the garden of the former British Consulate. In this house dating from the first half of the third century BC, a dining-room with a mosaic floor has been uncovered. Round the edges, a red band marks the area where the couches for the diners would have stood. The rosette medallion in the centre is made of little pebbles, just like the 'doormat' at the entrance. This technique is similar to that employed in mosaics found in strata of the same period in Macedonia.

beautiful scale pattern in *opus tessellatum*. In its centre is a medallion made of tiny tesserae only a few millimetres across in *opus vermiculatum*, containing the head of Medusa, who would protect the banqueters by turning would-be intruders to stone with her stare. We have not yet been able to determine the outer limits of this house on all sides, but in its present state of excavation it measures more than 200 square metres.

These two examples show clearly that the central districts, which must have been residential, were made up of large town houses which had nothing in common with the tall apartment blocks of Rome, but were similar to those of other eastern Mediterranean cities up to the third century AD. Even though one cannot draw firm conclusions from this about the other districts, where hardly any houses have been found among the sparse remains of earlier date, one still retains the impression that the urban landscape was dominated by dwellings with an extended ground-plan – a fact which will affect, at least provisionally, our estimate of the size of the population, as we shall see.

Two pieces of carved bone from a workshop of the fourth century AD: a maenad (above) and (left) a young man.

CHAPTER FOUR

The Seventh Wonder of the World

OPPOSITE: Upper part of an obelisk of Seti I, found during underwater excavations at the foot of Fort Qait Bey.

Fort Qait Bey, built by the Mamluk sultan Ashraf Qait Bey in 1477–80.

OPPOSITE PAGE: Upper part of the statue of a Ptolemaic queen as Isis. Kamal Abu el-Saadat first drew attention to her and persuaded the Egyptian Navy to hoist her on to dry land. At present she is at the Maritime Museum of Alexandria, waiting for somebody to find her lower legs so that she can be re-erected.

IT IS MARCH 1994: Asma el-Bakri, the Egyptian film-maker who has just finished shooting *Mendiants et Orgueilleux* ('Proud Beggars') after the novel by Albert Cossery, is making a film about the Graeco-Roman Museum at Alexandria. She wants to include some outdoor scenes illustrating the find contexts of the objects preserved in the museum. There are depictions of the famous lighthouse on coins and terracottas, but Asma el-Bakri has decided to take underwater shots of the remains at the foot of the Qait Bey Fort, which for several decades now have been regarded as those of the Seventh Wonder of the World. She has engaged cameramen and photographers who can dive. I join the expedition in the role of scientific adviser.

Of course, I knew that the Alexandrian archaeologist Kamal Abu el-Saadat had called attention to the importance of this site, and that in 1961 he had managed to persuade the Egyptian Navy to retrieve from the water the colossal statue of Isis in Aswan granite which can be admired today on the lawn of the Maritime Museum. In 1968, at the request of the Egyptian government, UNESCO had sent the British archaeologist Honor Frost to assess the importance of the site. Following her mission, she had published a report with drawings of the objects that lay under the water, in particular another colossal statue and a sphinx.

A few years later, in 1980, a team of Italian film-makers who were shooting a film about the Egyptian coast also did some diving on the Qait Bey site. They subsequently published an article in a specialist journal in which they described their astonishment at the impressiveness of the site and even went so far as to imagine that they had found themselves contemplating not only the remains of the Pharos but also those of Alexander's tomb!

The authors had got it into their heads that the Soma (literally 'the body' in Greek), as Alexander's tomb was called, had been built at the base of the Pharos. This was the only way they could explain to themselves the existence there of such imposing ruins. The relative ease with which research permits can be obtained from the Egyptian authorities at Alexandria has

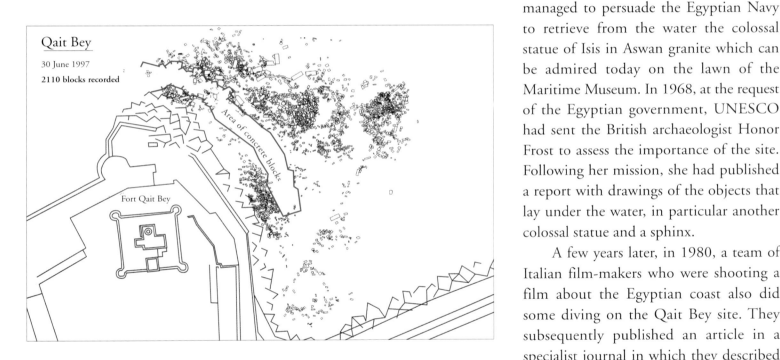

Qait Bey

30 June 1997

2110 blocks recorded

Area of concrete blocks

Fort Qait Bey

Plan of the underwater archaeological site at the foot of the Qait Bey Fort (as it was on 30 June 1997). On either side of the series of modern concrete blocks (outlined in blue), 2,110 ancient blocks have been mapped.

often encouraged enterprises which may seem to us in retrospect rather fanciful. This is true of an American expedition whose members claimed they could find both the Soma and the Pharos with the help of mediums. Although they confused ancient and modern remains in their attempts at identification, they did manage to dive down to the submerged ruins below Qait Bey and declare in their turn that they really were the remains of the Pharos!

I was present when Asma el-Bakri brought her little group to film the underwater footage. There wasn't a ripple on the sea. The wind was from the south and visibility was unusually good: from the surface one could see the blocks piled higgledy-piggledy eight metres (26 ft) below. We rarely had the chance to benefit from such clear water during the years of excavation that were to come.

It was with a feeling of surprise and wonder that we contemplated the hundreds of objects amassed over more than two hectares (5 acres), even though we were able to find no clue to the meaning or arrangement of this gigantic ruinfield. But the subsequent discovery of the torso of a colossal statue, and after that of some half-dozen bases designed to support statues of a similar size, and then of bodies of sphinxes beheaded by the backwash (as the neck is the weakest part of these stone monsters, it was only at a deeper level that we were able to discover, a year later, the only sphinx preserved intact) – all this was to be captured on film and in photographs by the divers, astonished and enraptured by the unexpected sight.

PREVIOUS PAGES: One of the blocks thought to be from the Pharos in the process of being lifted and brought on shore in 1995. It is one of two fragments of a door-frame in Aswan granite, measuring over 11 metres (36 ft) in height.

ABOVE: The Qait Bey excavations: A calcite sphinx of Psammetichus II (twenty-sixth dynasty, sixth century BC). Its head was found underneath its body.

Not far from the coast, I noticed and photographed an unusual structure of modern blocks on top of columns of Aswan granite. I mentioned it to Asma only once, on dry land: we were taking a stroll on the top of the fort when we saw a crane on a barge in the process of gingerly placing a concrete cube on the sea-bed. It was one of the twenty-ton blocks which were piled by the dozen against the breakwater which protects the Eastern Harbour.

When Asma realized that an unexplored ancient site was in the process of being buried in this way, her heart skipped a beat – as the Egyptian newspapers put it in their coverage of the incident, her cry of indignation reached Cairo! And the reaction was prompt: the authorities asked me to include the sea-bed in the rescue digs which I had so far restricted to the centre of the city. They knew that I had directed underwater excavations in Greece and off Cyprus; I had even started to train an Egyptian archaeologist there in this specialized work.

This proposition that I should conduct underwater excavations came, however, at a particularly bad moment. It was autumn and our funds were almost exhausted. I was on the point of declining the offer when I mentioned it to Nicolas Grimal, the director of the IFAO. I told him it was a heaven-sent proposition, but one I would have to turn down for lack of money. He asked me how much I needed. The actions of extremist groups had made Upper Egypt insecure and his expeditions had been cancelled, so he still had some funds left which he could put at my disposal. And that is how the first campaign of the Pharos excavation got under way.

In the process of reassembling the team of archaeologist-divers with whom I had worked on the discovery of the ancient harbours of Thasos, one of the northerly Greek islands, and of Amathus, near the modern town of Limassol on Cyprus, I asked two Egyptologists at the IFAO, Jean-Pierre Corteggiani and Georges Soukiassian, if they would like to be involved in the project. Fortunately, they both accepted: we were to find numerous

An archaeologist in diving gear making a drawing under water of a floral capital made of granite and dating from the end of the Ptolemaic period.

OVERLEAF: A diver measuring one of the blocks belonging to the Pharos. It is part of a door-frame in Aswan pink granite and is more than 5 metres (16½ ft) high.

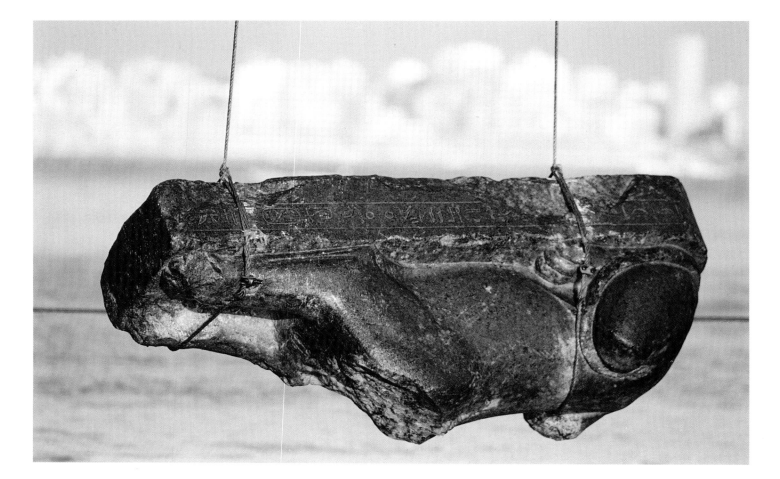

monuments covered in hieroglyphs, and their collaboration was to prove invaluable, or, rather, absolutely indispensable in this Graeco-Roman city, which until now had held little attraction for Egyptologists.

AS SOON AS ONE PUTS ONE'S HEAD under the water around Qait Bey, one begins to feel dizzy at the sight of the 3,000 or so architectural blocks which carpet the sea-bed. The number of columns and column fragments runs into hundreds. The latest of these, with a modest diameter of about 60 centimetres (2 ft), are made of Proconnesian marble from the Princes' Islands in the Sea of Marmara between Istanbul and the Dardanelles. These quarries are in the process of being excavated. From the fourth century BC onwards, they were exploited in an almost industrial way and supplied the whole Mediterranean basin with an easily recognizable, beautiful white marble with grey veins. The capitals and sarcophagi that are still being found at Alexandria are often made of it. The bigger columns are

A sphinx from the reign of Psammetichus II, captured as a floating crane lifts it from the underwater surroundings in which it has spent the past fifteen centuries or so.

Three thousand building blocks

PREVIOUS PAGES: A diver face to face with a sphinx. In this photograph, which has been reproduced world-wide since 1995, an Egyptian diver is drawing the only sphinx to have retained its head on its body. It is made of grey granite and appears to date from the reign of Ramses II, according to the hieroglyphs on its base.

carved from Aswan granite and can reach unusually large proportions: one of them has a diameter of more than 2.3 metres (7½ ft), which is comparable with the top of Pompey's Pillar. We also found on the sea-bed several column bases with moulded profile, and some Corinthian capitals in pink or grey granite, which would fit the other end of such columns.

Among these smooth shafts, half-a-dozen papyrus columns caught our attention. Some of them bore the cartouche of Ramses II. We were suddenly transported back in time: they date from nine centuries before the foundation of Alexandria!

Half-a-dozen papyrus columns have been found on the underwater site of Qait Bey. Several carry cartouches of Ramses II (thirteenth century BC). They almost certainly come from Heliopolis and have been recut; they were probably used in the masonry of an Alexandrian monument.

Similarly, fragments of three obelisks were found in the same area. They belong to Seti I, the father of Ramses II. Of one, three fragments which fit together and two bits of the base have been found; of the other, only one fragment. Both obelisks are made of calcite, and they appear to be a pair. On them the figure of the pharaoh can be seen in sunken relief bringing offerings to the deities of Heliopolis. The third obelisk is made of Aswan pink granite. On two of its sides the pharaoh is represented as the Seth animal, a kind of tapir that does not belong to the native fauna of Egypt;

on the other two sides Seti is depicted as a sphinx with a human face before a deity.

The sphinxes proved to be even more numerous than the obelisks: we have catalogued twenty-five of them in three excavation campaigns. They are all different and made of various stones: calcite, pink granite, grey granite. There is also a big difference in their ages: the oldest carries the cartouche of Sesostris III and so dates from the twelfth dynasty (nineteenth century BC); the most recent dates from the reign of Psammetichus II, a pharaoh of the twenty-sixth dynasty (early sixth century BC). They are a heterogeneous collection and obviously do not make up an avenue or anything of that kind. They have all been taken from another site, and those with an inscription show where they come from: it is again Heliopolis.

Some of these sphinxes, which are in a good state of preservation, were doubtless part of the embellishment of the Ptolemaic city, just like the obelisks, the prime examples of which, 'Cleopatra's Needles', I shall be discussing later on. Other specimens of these fantastic quadrupeds, on the other hand, had been carved up – one might almost say butchered – and must have been reused in the masonry of a building.

These numerous products of the pharaonic period – sphinxes, obelisks and papyrus columns – do not make any significant difference to what we already know about the history of Alexandria and its foundation by Alexander the Great in 331 BC, but they bear eloquent testimony to the 'borrowings' made from the sanctuary at Heliopolis, first by the Ptolemies, then by the Roman emperors. They join other finds with pharaonic features discovered during the excavations on dry land and give the Greek city of Alexandria a special character of its own: the city must in parts, have had an Egyptian feel, with sphinxes lining the streets and with obelisks towering in front of the temples and in public open spaces. Thus archaeology has confirmed the testimony of ancient authors such as Pliny the Elder, who in the mid-first century AD drew up a list of the obelisks transported to Alexandria.

Detail of a scene in sunken relief on the base of a calcite obelisk. Ramses II's father, Seti I, can be recognized, presenting offerings to the deities of Heliopolis.

Detail from an obelisk of Seti I, made of Aswan pink granite, showing a sphinx with a kind of tapir's head. It is a rebus: 'Set', represented by the animal of the god Seth, Osiris' brother, and 'i' by two hieroglyphs in the form of feathers beneath him.

One of the most remarkable objects we found on the sea-bed is the torso of a colossal male statue in Aswan pink granite. Preserved from the base of the neck to mid-thigh, it measures 4.55 metres (15 ft). It obviously represents a pharaoh, but the execution leaves no room for doubt: it dates from the Ptolemaic period and must be one of the Ptolemies portrayed in the costume of a traditional Egyptian ruler. Unfortunately, there is no inscription to tell us who he is.

This statue is reminiscent of the one that the Egyptian Navy raised in 1961 at the insistence of Kamal Abu el-Saadat, which remained for many years at the foot of Pompey's Pillar, before being moved in 1991 to the garden of the Maritime Museum. There, on the lawn, the two contiguous fragments of this giant Isis may be inspected. She, too, is made of Aswan pink granite, and preserved from the top of the head to mid-leg. In this state, she measures 7 metres (23 ft); and if a crown with the solar disk between the cow horns of Hathor that was found on the sea-bed fits her head, she must have been more than 12 metres (40 ft) tall when complete. This is about the same size as our male colossus would originally have been. Moreover, Honor Frost has informed me that Kamal Abu el-Saadat found the two statues lying side by side, just below their respective bases. This means that they were found *in situ* and that they must have stood on this

Three-dimensional reconstruction of a colossal statue of a Ptolemy as pharaoh. On the left, the four separate parts of the statue; on the right, the same parts reassembled. The weight of the fragments (23 tons in total; the torso alone weighs 17 tons) makes it difficult to rejoin them physically. The technique used here, thanks to sponsorship from EDF, has made the reconstruction of the colossus a much easier task for our restorers.

spot in antiquity. They probably represent a royal couple, a Ptolemy at the side of his wife, a queen dressed as Isis, just as on the coins of the period.

Besides these two colossi, the remains of three further statues of a similar size lay beneath the water: two heads of pharaohs with Hellenistic features, and a female bust. We have counted six bases which could belong to as many statues: it may be concluded that three royal couples stood there in antiquity. The ancient authors, foremost among them Strabo, locate the lighthouse of Alexandria at the eastern end of the island of Pharos – in just the place where the statues were found – and it can be assumed that the Ptolemies chose to erect these colossal effigies of themselves at the foot of its tower as an act of propaganda that obliged every sailor and traveller arriving by sea in the Eastern Harbour, the Megas Limen (Greek: Great Harbour), to enter the country by sailing past these statues, which with their bases must have been about 12 metres (40 ft) high. They combined their effigies with the monument which was the emblem of their city, and clothed them in a pharaonic form to show that they were not only the lords of a great Greek city, but also the sovereigns of all Egypt.

Other architectural elements of the Qait Bey site merit attention, in particular some flagstones, and some door-jambs and lintels, all in Aswan pink granite, which are also remarkable for their size: the biggest are more than

OPPOSITE PAGE: Head of Aswan granite belonging to a colossal statue of a Ptolemy represented as a pharaoh, identifiable by his headdress, the *nemes*. The discovery of other heads makes it very probable that he is one of a series of colossal statues of royal couples erected at the foot of the Pharos.

LEFT: The inscribed band on the base of Pharaoh Psammetichus II's calcite sphinx.

BELOW LEFT: The Egyptologist Jean-Pierre Corteggiani cleaning a fragment of a calcite obelisk of Seti I. The participation of Egyptologists who can dive has meant that the inscriptions on pharaonic finds, the large number of which was one of the surprises on this excavation, can be deciphered under water. The drawing (below) was done by the architect Isabelle Hairy and is a reconstruction of one of the two calcite obelisks of Seti I.

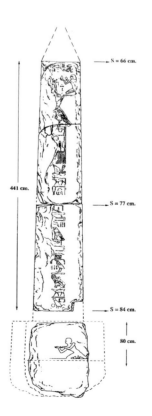

Bust of a colossal female statue in Aswan pink granite, lying on the sea-bed. She was raised in 1995.

OPPOSITE PAGE: The same statue in the open air, showing the fine folds of her garment over a shapely bosom. Stylistic features suggest that this is a work of the Hellenistic period. Between her breasts there may be the traces of an Isis-knot, indicating that she is a Ptolemaic queen represented as Isis.

11.5 metres (38 ft) high and weigh more than 70 tons. These gigantic blocks lie in a line starting at the fort and running from south-west to north-east, and some of them are broken into two, or even three, pieces, which shows that they fell from quite a height. In view of the location the ancient writers give for the lighthouse, and taking into consideration the technical difficulty of moving such large objects, it is probable that these are parts of the Pharos itself which lie where they were flung by a particularly violent earthquake. Admittedly, Strabo says the lighthouse was built of white stone – doubtless the local limestone – but it is likely that for the parts which needed extra reinforcement, such as the window- and door-frames, the builders had recourse to a more solid building material that could be cut into larger units. They resorted to their ancestral skill in the cutting of granite, thus combining Egyptian tradition with Greek building techniques.

The Pharos

OPPOSITE PAGE: This model, in the Maritime Museum at Alexandria, was made a few years ago by an Egyptian craftsman after Hermann Thiersch's reconstruction on paper in the early twentieth century.

ABOVE: Terracotta lantern of the Ptolemaic period, representing the Pharos of Alexandria. The holes which helped to draw the flame of the lamp placed inside it represent the windows of the Pharos, while the lines incised in the clay mark the courses of masonry. The three tiers of the tower are clearly distinguished.

THE SEVENTH WONDER had undergone many vicissitudes since its construction at the beginning of the third century BC. It must have been the work of the first Ptolemy and was inaugurated by his son, Ptolemy Philadelphus, in 283 BC, having taken a dozen years to build. The tower had three tiers, according to the reconstruction drawing by Hermann Thiersch, the learned German scholar and author of a book which has served as a reference work since 1909. Thiersch used depictions on coins, mosaics in Roman buildings in Libya and Jordan, even one on a wall in St Mark's at Venice. (In the eleventh century AD, when this basilica was consecrated to house the relics of the apostle St Mark, which had been stolen from Alexandria by Venetian merchants, the Pharos was still standing.) He also used lanterns, like the one in the Graeco-Roman Museum, and gems. There is obviously no lack of depictions of the Pharos: for instance, a little vase with a lighthouse on it, found at Beghram, north of Kabul, was doubtless brought back as a souvenir by a traveller returning from Alexandria, like the little metal Eiffel towers that nowadays adorn living rooms the world over. It is only a pity that such representations do not provide very precise details of its design, and particularly of the arrangement of the lantern, for instance.

This monumental edifice is represented in all the records as a tower with three tiers: first a quadrangular one, then an octagonal, and finally a cylindrical one. The entrance was approached by a long ramp with vaulted arcades, and a spiral staircase led to perhaps fifty service rooms and also enabled pack animals to bring firewood up to the third tier to feed the fire kept burning at the top. We do not, on the other hand, possess many descriptions by ancient writers: the most eloquent are by Arab travellers, who admired this architectural masterpiece. However, one often has to reject their testimony, as they combine the most precise detail with wild fantasy. Some of them, like Abu el-Haggag el-Andalusi, give measurements which result in a reconstruction of very different proportions from that of Thiersch, who did not know this author, as the manuscripts of his work were only discovered twenty-five years after Thiersch's study appeared. The higher up the tower we go, the less we know about it; and this vagueness becomes an almost total state of ignorance when we come to the lantern.

This tier had, in any case, already been destroyed by the medieval period, and so the Arab accounts must be treated with appropriate caution. What is one to believe when they talk of a mirror, or even of a huge lens designed to increase the range and visibility of the light? The arrangement as reconstructed by Thiersch also leaves one a little perplexed: how could a hot fire have been kept burning under a cupola supported on columns without the

FIRMIAVICTORAQVEV
LXV

Detail of an early Christian sarcophagus (third century AD) showing a ship arriving within sight of a port (perhaps Ostia) and of a lighthouse (Rome, Museum of Roman Civilization).

heat cracking the stonework? How could the fire have been roofed in and surrounded with columns without their limiting its brightness and range?

If, however, one locates the beacon right on top of the tower, in the open, what is one to do with the statue of a deity mentioned in several texts? For a long time it was believed that he was Poseidon, the lord of the waves; but then a papyrus was discovered. It is preserved in the Louvre and contains verses by the poet Poseidippos of Pella, who lived at the Alexandrian court in the third century BC. They have convinced historians that the lighthouse was crowned by a statue of Zeus the Saviour. However, new evidence is still coming to light, and the suggestion has recently been made that there was not just one statue, but two: Zeus accompanied by Poseidon. These are just a couple of examples to show how difficult it is to solve the technical problems associated with the presence and exact position of one (or two) statue(s) above the beacon.

The dedicatory inscription (the wording of which we know) does not mention these statues: 'Sostratos of Knidos, son of Dexiphanes [has dedicated this monument] to the gods for the protection of sailors.' This

Sostratos, a person of note whom one meets elsewhere, making dedications in the sanctuaries of Apollo at Delphi and on Delos, is certainly not simply an architect, as he has often been portrayed, but undoubtedly the project's sponsor and the person who dedicated the Pharos to the 'gods'. This is the usual *epiklesis* (title) of the Dioscuri, the twin sons of Zeus and Leda and step-brothers of Clytemnestra and Helen of Troy. Among their various attributes they were the patron deities of youths in the gymnasium and the protectors of seafarers.

The first modern scholar to have made use of this dedication (which is quoted by Lucian of Samosata, who lived in Athens in the second century AD) was J. A. Letronne, more than a century ago. From his study in Paris, he imagined the two statues of the Dioscuri on top of the Pharos. It is definitely getting uncomfortably full up there – Zeus, Poseidon, and now the Dioscuri; that's a lot of statues for such a small area! Obviously it would be simpler to imagine a beacon open to the sky on the very top, and to send all the statues down to the base of the monument. That would explain the scene on a gem which has recently been studied, on which the Pharos is easily recognizable. At its base two deities face each other: on the left Isis Pharia holds a sail that billows in the wind; on the right Poseidon brandishes his trident. Our own discoveries have shown, as I explained above, that colossal statues of at least three royal couples were erected in this situation. One could conclude that these statues of deities stood alongside the effigies of the pharaoh-kings, who, like them, were divine, so that they might be seen in this strategic position by everybody entering or leaving the Eastern Harbour.

Mosaic in St Mark's basilica, Venice (thirteenth century), telling the story of the saint, who brought the gospel to the Alexandrians. He is seen arriving at Alexandria, indicated by a depiction of the Pharos, which was still standing and in use when this mosaic was made.

The Well of Wonders: the Pharos of Alexandria: fresco by Nicolas Schiel, 1669. Convent of Novacella, Italy.

Mosaic representing an ancient lighthouse, from the Square of the Corporations at Ostia.

Even if our researches (and it must be stressed that they are still in progress and that their results are provisional) do not permit us to paint a picture very different from that proposed by Thiersch, the archaeological data have given the lighthouse a new appearance. We can no longer regard it as a work purely in the Greek style: its builders will have borrowed from the pharaonic tradition. The Ptolemies were great builders of temples in Upper Egypt, and almost all the sanctuaries people visit today – Philae, Esna, Edfu, Kom Ombo and others – bear witness to their architectural feats. At Alexandria, Aswan granite was used, along with the skill and the trained workers it requires, at any rate for the parts of the lighthouse building that needed reinforcing. It is hard to imagine such parts in marble, let alone limestone. Rather than importing marble from the Greek islands, the Ptolemies tended to exploit their own quarries. To judge from the amount of coloured stone found in the excavations in the city centre, people in Egypt derived pleasure from using contrasting colours, including pink, green and black, and decorating their buildings with them.

The lighthouse of Alexandria is one of the world's longest-serving functional monuments. No fewer than seventeen centuries passed between its construction and its collapse (third century BC to fourteenth century AD), during which time it served as a guide to sailors approaching the coast of Egypt. During the course of almost two millennia it experienced many vicissitudes, and when one considers to what degree its position exposed it to the winds, to storms (which can be very violent at Alexandria) and even to tidal waves, like the one which affected the eastern Mediterranean in AD 365, one becomes convinced that it was an exceptionally well-constructed building. Only earthquakes got the better of it: between 320 and 1303, twenty-two were severe enough to be mentioned by ancient, and after them by Arab, writers.

In 796 the lighthouse lost its third tier, and a century later Sultan Ibn Tulun (868–84) installed a mosque with a dome on top of it. In 950 and 956, parts of the surface cracked and it was reduced in height by 22 metres (72 ft). In 1261 it was again hit by an earthquake and another section collapsed. The Arabs admired it and did their best to look after it. We have quite lot of information about repairs: in 1272 Sultan Salah el-Din (Saladin) undertook restoration work which enabled the building to survive until the fourteenth century. On 8 August 1303 a big earthquake shook the whole eastern Mediterranean. It was felt in Greece and the Levant, and also affected the Delta. Alexandria was hit. A medieval maritime map preserved

at Montpellier inscribes beside the city the date of the quake and notes that the lighthouse was totally destroyed. As Ibn Taghribardi wrote: 'the princes who occupy themselves with pious works spent a long time repairing the damage done in the schools, the mosques and even the lighthouse.'

Even so, the latter must have been in a pitiful condition, and the first half of the fourteenth century proved fatal for it. The Maghrebi traveller Ibn Battuta paid two visits to Alexandria: on his first, in 1329, he was able to climb the ramp and reach the door of the tower; in 1346 he could no longer get near it – the lighthouse was in ruins. It was to remain in this state for a little more than a century, before the Mamluk sultan Qait Bey decided to construct on its ruins the fort which still stands there today.

The memory of this extraordinary tower remained alive: in the sixteenth century, two centuries after it had vanished, Sultan el-Ghury commissioned a model of the city of Alexandria and had the Pharos included in it, even though Qait Bey's fort had been built more than a hundred years earlier. Long after its disappearance the Pharos continued to occupy a place in the memory of both Arab and Western authors – one has only to call to mind the numerous engravings which depict it in a more or less fantastic fashion and sometimes even transform it into a veritable Tower of Babel.

Alexandrian bronze coin of the second century AD, with Isis Pharia holding a sail in front of the Pharos. The ramp leading to the door of the square tier can be seen. Above it is another tier, of uncertain form. On the corners are tritons blowing conches. The tower is surmounted by a statue with the left arm bent towards the body and the right outstretched.

Engraving of the Pharos as reconstructed by Monneret de Villard. It shows it as it was in the Arab period, with a base resembling that of the future Fort Qait Bey, surmounted first by a tower with many windows; then a kind of openwork bell tower or minaret, and finally a third tier crowned by a dome. Pennants flutter at the top of the first tier, while torches smoke on the corners of the upper tier.

CHAPTER FIVE

The Sarapeion and Pompey's Pillar

OPPOSITE: Basalt statue of an Apis bull. Dedicated by the emperor Hadrian, according to the inscription on the pillar supporting its belly, it was discovered at the end of the last century in a crypt of the Sarapeion. The statue is proof of the durability of the cult of the old pharaonic deity of Memphis, still venerated in this Alexandrian sanctuary in the middle of the second century AD.

Pompey's Pillar at Alexandria. As this watercolour by Vivant Denon shows, people used to fly a kite up to it, attaching a thin cord which they gradually replaced with thicker cords, in order to climb to the top. This climb was all the rage in the nineteenth century.

Second-century coin from the Alexandrian mint, showing the temple of Sarapis. In a Greek architectural setting of columns surmounted by Corinthian capitals and a triangular pediment, stands the statue of Sarapis, facing to the right. He leans on a spear and wears the *modius*, by which he is immediately identifiable. This coin belongs to the period of Hadrian and shows the temple rebuilt by this Egyptophile emperor.

The Temple of Sarapis

OPPOSITE PAGE: Bronze head of the Emperor Hadrian found at Qena. The emperor liked both Greece and Egypt, and particularly Alexandria. He rebuilt the Sarapeion, reconstructing the temple and dedicating the basalt bull now in the Graeco-Roman Museum. He also built a library which housed the city archives.

P TOLEMY I DESIRED FOR POLITICAL REASONS to create a harmonious relationship between the Greek immigrants he had encouraged to come to Alexandria from all over the eastern Mediterranean and the native Egyptian population, which continued through the centuries to form the demographic majority in the country. To achieve this he resorted to religion. In a dream he had a vision of a deity who demanded to be adopted by the Alexandrians. After various complications, which the ancient authors elaborate in copious detail, Ptolemy sent for the statue of a god venerated by the inhabitants of the distant city of Sinope on the south shore of the Black Sea. At Alexandria a temple was built and dedicated to this new deity, Sarapis, who was to become under the Ptolemies and for a long time afterwards the symbol of Alexandrian religion. Never had the invention of a completely new cult by a political power been so successful: it spread all over Egypt, and then throughout the Mediterranean. Soon every Greek city was building its own Sarapeion. Even Rome admitted the cult: one of the districts of the imperial capital was named after the god, and at the end of the first century AD, under Domitian, he received the ultimate accolade and was included among the gods worshipped on the Capitol. What a remarkable career for Ptolemy I's dream-child!

ALTHOUGH THE CULT OF SARAPIS had an immediate impact on the Greeks and shortly afterwards on the Romans, its success with the Egyptians was much more limited. The well-organized local priesthood continued to tend the people's ardent love for their ancestral gods. Ptolemy, however, had thought up a wise measure which ought to have suited both ethnic groups. The new god assumed Egyptian features: he tried to replace Osiris by becoming the new husband of Isis, while his son by her, Harpocrates, took the place of Horus. Moreover, his power found further legitimation in the continuation of the cult of the Apis bull, to which the Ptolemies were to accord special status for the rest of their dynasty.

Sarapis also drew inspiration from the Memphite god of the dead, Osir-Apis, the designation of the deceased Apis bull who was worshipped at Memphis in the pharaonic period. Proof of this appeared at the end of the nineteenth century, when a lifesize statue of a bull in black basalt was discovered in a crypt of the Sarapeion at Alexandria. It was an offering made by the Emperor Hadrian. It is also shown by the foundation tablets of Ptolemy III, on which the 'Sarapis' of the Greek text is rendered by 'Osor-Apis' in the hieroglyphic version. In a similar fashion, Sarapis borrowed attributes and powers from several gods of the Greek pantheon: from Zeus, king of

the gods, from Asklepios (Latin: Aesculapius), the healer god, and from Hades, the god of the Underworld. This is referred to in the literary sources, including Plutarch and Tacitus. 'He is believed by many people to be Aesculapius', writes Tacitus, 'because he heals the sick; by some to be Osiris, the oldest god in those parts; by a large number to be Jupiter as he is master of all things; but by most people to be Father Dis, either because he displays attributes obviously connected with the Underworld, or for some more obscure reasons.'[20] This bearded god, easily recognizable by the corkscrew curls on his forehead, united in his person all kinds of benign powers, which were to make him one of the great healer-gods of the Hellenistic and Roman periods. His cult statue, brought from Sinope with a great deal of difficulty, was to be housed in a grand sanctuary in a key position, on one of the free-standing rocky outcrops the Alexandrians termed 'akropoleis'. The location had symbolic value – as we have seen, the quarter of Rhakotis had once been occupied by a fishing village (its structures must have been simple, as no archaeological trace of them remains).

It was in this spot, which served as a sea-mark for sailors approaching the coast and was clearly visible on all sides from the town below, that Ptolemy I started to build the temple of Sarapis. It was to be enlarged, or rather reconstructed on a more ambitious scale, by his grandson Ptolemy III, as the foundation tablets found in one of the corners of the sanctuary have shown. The building must have been badly damaged during the Jewish uprisings under Trajan in AD 116 – badly enough at any rate for Hadrian to build a new temple. It is this temple which appears on the coins of Alexandria in the second century. On them one can recognize Sarapis, crowned with the *modius* (measuring basket), between two columns of a pedimented temple.

The only existing descriptions of the temple are late and come from writers of the fourth century. According to one of them, Rufinus, a flight of a hundred steps led to an enclosure with porticoes, inside which were the living-quarters of the priests and, in the centre, the square temple. This latter housed a colossal statue of Sarapis in wood and metal, and the walls themselves were covered in precious metal. 'A very small window had been installed on the side where the sun rises' writes Rufinus, 'in such a way that on the day on which it was customary to bring the statue of the Sun to greet Serapis (the time having been carefully calculated), just as the statue was coming in, a sun beam shining straight through this window lit up the mouth and lips of Serapis, so that it seemed to the watching crowd that Serapis was being greeted with a kiss by the sun.'[21]

Rufinus is a valuable witness: he lived in Alexandria at the time of the

destruction of the temple at the end of the fourth century. As a Christian propagandist, he shows no indulgence towards the pagan cults; quite to the contrary – he tries to explain how the priests of the Sarapeion abuse the credulity of the faithful. His description of the cunningly installed opening designed to catch the first rays of the sun helps us to understand a scene on Alexandrian coins of the second century. On these one sees a Greek temple with a triangular pediment supported on four columns and with a large central door flanked by two smaller ones. In the tympanum one can make out a little bust, doubtless that of Sarapis, with the *modius* on his head. Through a window installed above the central door one can clearly recognize the same god: it is the head and shoulders of the great cult statue, which could apparently be seen from outside through this opening, and which must be the one mentioned by Rufinus. The sacred kiss was a source of energy for the god.

Pharaonic religion was familiar with this kind of solar recharging of divinities. It was practised in many sanctuaries, especially in the Ptolemaic temples of Upper Egypt. At Esna, Edfu and Dendera, as well as plenty of other places, this ceremony was conducted in a kiosk at the entrance of the sanctuary. At the Sarapeion some of the clergy must have been native Egyptians, as the statues of Egyptian priests found in its precinct suggest, and there must also have been a connection between certain aspects of the cult of Sarapis and pharaonic cult.

Rufinus adds: 'There was yet another instance of this sort of trickery. The natural property of the magnetic stone is said to be to attract iron and draw it to itself. The statue of the Sun had been made by a craftsman of very fine iron to the following end: a stone with the property I have just mentioned of attracting iron had been fixed in the panelling of the ceiling, and when the statue was placed in exactly the right position beneath it, it drew the

Marble bust of Sarapis.
The god invented by Ptolemy I can be recognized by his mature appearance, his long beard, the five corkscrew curls on his forehead and his *modius* headdress: this inverted vase-shape decorated with leaves is a symbol of prosperity. The deity borrowed his characteristic features and his powers from Osiris, Aesculapius, Hades and Zeus. Graeco-Roman Museum, Alexandria.

BELOW: Alabaster bust of a Hermosarapis. The clearly identifiable Ptolemaic deity is here associated with the Greek god Hermes, whose little wings adorn his forehead.

ABOVE: Statue of the god Sarapis in sycomore-fig wood, from the small town of Philadelphia in the Fayum. The remains of white stucco with traces of colour are still visible. The body of the seated statue is made of a single piece of wood; the arms are attachments.

iron towards itself by virtue of its natural force, and it seemed to the people as if the statue had risen and now remained suspended in the air. And so that the deceit should not be given away by the statue falling down abruptly, the ministrants of deception would say, "the Sun has risen to say farewell to Serapis and return to his own realm".'[22]

The veracity of this account has sometimes been questioned, but there are several reasons for believing that Rufinus is describing something he has actually seen at Alexandria. There is a similar description in another author of the same period, Quodvultdeus: 'At Alexandria, the following diabolical representation was to be found in the temple of Serapis: an iron quadriga, which was neither supported on a base, nor attached to the wall by any brackets, remained suspended in the air and gave to mortal eyes the incredible impression that the gods were coming to succour them. In fact, a magnet (a stone which by its power holds in suspension any object of iron held towards it) had been fixed at this point in the ceiling and held the whole contraption suspended.'[23]

One might suspect the second author of copying the first, but parallels show that the same procedure was used in other sanctuaries: at Alexandria it was also employed in the Arsinoeion, the temple which Ptolemy II had started to build after the death of his wife and sister, Arsinoe II, in 270 BC. This is how Pliny the Elder describes the mechanism of the cult statue: 'The architect Dinochares had begun to use lodestone for constructing the vaulting in the Temple of Arsinoe at Alexandria, so that the iron statue contained in it might have the appearance of being suspended in mid air; but the project was interrupted by his own death and that of King Ptolemy who had ordered the work to be done in honour of his sister.'[24]

Claudian's description of a *hieros gamos* (sacred marriage) is similar: he says that a statue of Venus in magnetic stone drew to it an iron statue of Mars in the course of a nuptial ceremony presided over by a priest.[25]

There certainly seem to have been a number of similar devices which lend credibility to Rufinus' description. They may be regarded as an achievement of the Alexandrian engineers who interested themselves in mechanics, experimenting with pneumatic phenomena and applying their skill to the effects of magnetism, even if it is hard to see how they kept the magnetic flux under control. The end of the text quoted from Rufinus, however, shows that accidents could happen!

There is almost nothing left of the temple today. It was destroyed right down to the foundations by Christians at the end of the fourth century. Historians relate that Bishop Theophilus sent out his troops to put an end

Manuscript showing Bishop Theophilus symbolically surmounting the statue of Sarapis as the Sarapeion is destroyed in AD 391. Vienna, Kunsthistorisches Museum.

Pompey's Pillar

OPPOSITE PAGE: Drawing of Pompey's Pillar by L.F. Cassas (1784). The drawing of the top of the capital (top left) shows that Cassas, like the scholars who later came with Napoleon, took the trouble to climb the column, probably with the help of a rope ladder.

ONE OF THESE SUBTERRANEAN GALLERIES leads beneath the base of a gigantic column which still stands upright on the site today – indeed, it is the only feature still standing. This monolith of Aswan granite is the biggest such monument in the Graeco-Roman world. The shaft is 30 metres (98 ft) high and has a diameter of 2.7 metres (9 ft) at the base and 2.3 metres (7½ ft) at the summit. It stands on a high base with a moulded profile, which appears to rest on a collection of reused building material. Through a small opening made in the modern cement with which it was repaired a few years ago, one can see a block which is definitely part of an obelisk with a hieroglyphic inscription naming Pharaoh Tuthmosis II. This is yet another instance of the removal to Alexandria of remains of the abandoned sanctuary of Heliopolis. As the plinth of the base had to be repaired, we have to turn to old engravings, in particular those of F. L. Norden (1738), L. F. Cassas (1784) and David Roberts (1846): the column appears to be perched on a motley assortment of foundations, which it overhangs considerably. This apparent instability is astonishing, especially considering that the column has defied the earthquakes which so severely affected the city's other monuments, in particular the Pharos. Pompey's Pillar is, in fact, the only ancient monument to remain standing in the whole of Alexandria.

The name 'Pompey's Pillar' is a misnomer, invented by travellers who were led astray by the constant desire to establish links between the monuments they discovered and the ancient texts they had read before embarking on their tours. For a long time people related the story that Caesar erected the column in honour of his old enemy Pompey. After his defeat at Pharsalos in Thessaly (16 August 48 BC), Pompey had taken to flight and had arrived off the coast of Egypt. Did he count on gaining the support of the Alexandrians? Nobody will ever know, because Theodotos, the regent of Ptolemy XIII (the ten-year-old king, who shared the throne with his seventeen-year-old sister, Cleopatra VII), in the belief that he was doing Caesar a favour, had Pompey beheaded as soon as he disembarked, and gave orders that this trophy should be laid at Caesar's feet. Far from being agreeable to the master of Rome, however, this sight reminded him that the man who had just been assassinated was also his son-in-law. This incident inspired some travellers to make conjectures about the location of Pompey's tomb: since it had to be found, and as the column was the only monument of ancient Alexandria still standing, they decided that that was where they would surely find what they were looking for.

In reality, Caesar never set eyes on the famous pillar, for the simple

of Alexandria. That is, unless (if one agrees with P. M. Fraser) these fragments were recovered in 1785 by the draughtsman L.F. Cassas and are now in France: 'Choiseul-Gouffier possesses two fragments of a colossal porphyry statue found by Monsieur Cassas beside the sea and brought to France by Admiral Trouguet, then ship's captain. One of these seems to be the upper part of the thigh of a warrior wearing a cuirass. M. Cassas thought at first that the figure to which this part belonged could have crowned the column; but judging by the length of this fragment, it would have been about 7 m high (21ft 6in), or a third the height of the shaft, and consequently obviously too big, since we know from similar examples that the statues on monuments of this kind measured only about an eighth of their height.'[27]

Fraser concludes from this text that Cassas had got hold of the remains of the statue thrown into the sea by Rotoli. But other porphyry statues have been found in the city, for example the headless colossus seated on an imposing throne which presides over a room in the Graeco-Roman Museum. At any rate, whether the fragments of the Diocletian from Pompey's Pillar are now in the Megas Limen (Great Harbour) or in France, the statue did remain in place until the fifth century at least, as the Sepphoris mosaic shows. Ironically, the effigy of the emperor who ordered the bloody persecution of the Christians at the beginning of the fourth century survived the sack of the Sarapeion by Bishop Theophilus in 391.

OPPOSITE PAGE: In the foreground, a sphinx of Ramses II, taken from the sanctuary at Heliopolis to adorn the surroundings of the Sarapeion. Behind it is Pompey's Pillar.

Pompey's Pillar seen from the gardens of the archaeological park of the Sarapeion.

CHAPTER SIX

The Caesareum

OPPOSITE: One of Cleopatra's Needles, which remained standing until its removal by the Americans in 1879, as drawn for the *Description de l'Egypte*.

The shores of the Eastern Harbour with the Tower of the Romans and one of the two Cleopatra's Needles. The subsidence that has altered the ground level at Alexandria has led to considerable erosion on the coast. The obelisks which used to mark the entrance of the Caesareum are now on the coast, whereas in antiquity they must have been a good 100 metres (110 yds) away from it.

'Cleopatra's Needles', obelisks
originally erected by Pharaoh
Tuthmosis III in the temple of Re
at Heliopolis and later brought by
Augustus to Alexandria to mark the
entrance of the Caesareum, the
sanctuary dedicated to the imperial
cult. These two monuments are the
ones most often represented in
travellers' drawings. Below: an
engraving by David Roberts (1846).
Opposite page: an engraving by
Fredrick L. Norden (1737).

Excavations in the vicinity of the Caesareum

the protector of sailors or *epibaterios*. It also served as a landmark for seafarers entering the Eastern Harbour (Megas Limen). As Philo wrote, it was 'full of dedicated offerings, covered all around with pictures and statues and objects of silver and of gold', which doubtless included tokens of gratitude from sailors for the deity who had protected them, for example an ex-voto of a captain on an altar found during work on the foundations of the modern synagogue: 'Lucius Tonneius Anteros [has dedicated this altar] to Fair Voyage, for the safety of his ship, *Nikastarte*. In year 43 of Caesar [Augustus], on the twenty-first of Mechir.'

The architecture

Philo's description enables us to imagine the architectural layout of the temple: a huge open court surrounded by stoas that must have served as the outer walls of the sanctuary, just as at the Sarapeion. The rooms in the stoas must have housed books in the much same way as the other libraries in Alexandria; and some of them could have served as assembly rooms. In the open space between the stoas and the temple were the 'sacred groves and the open-air rooms' – but it is difficult to reconstruct the arrangement and function of the latter.

Finally, the temple proper in the centre of the enclosure was presumably built in the Greek style, if one can go by the scanty remains found by Napoleon's scholars. According to Saint-Genis, it would even have been built in the Doric order: 'But one can no longer recognize anything, at any rate not with certainty, of this temple of Caesar. One can however see, a few paces away and also on the seashore, some ruins which form the base of an Arab building and belong to a structure of the Greek or Roman period: one can make out the capitals of some engaged columns which belong to the Doric order. Their shafts rise from the sea-bed. And that is all one can really attribute to the Caesareum.'[29]

IN 1992–3, I CONDUCTED TWO EXCAVATIONS in the vicinity of the Caesareum: one on the site of the former Majestic Cinema, the other on that of the Billiardo Palace. On the first site, a long wall came to light at the bottom of a trial trench. It is constructed of large blocks laid as headers and can be dated by coins to the end of the first century BC. Its orientation is the same as that of the streets running east–west on Mahmud el-Falaki's grid plan (nineteenth century; see pp. 22–3) and it is contemporary with the Caesareum, but it is impossible to say to what part of the sanctuary it could belong. One of the finds at the Billiardo aroused our interest – a column

The Caesareum

The shores of the Eastern Harbour with the Tower of the Romans and one of the two Cleopatra's Needles. The subsidence that has altered the ground level at Alexandria has led to considerable erosion on the coast. The obelisks which used to mark the entrance of the Caesareum are now on the coast, whereas in antiquity they must have been a good 100 metres (110 yds) away from it.

ANOTHER REMARKABLE MONUMENT is the Caesareum. It is not as old as the other sanctuaries or public buildings discussed in this book – for example, the Pharos or the tomb of Alexander – but it so quickly became an important part, not just of the landscape but also of the life of the city, that it cannot be omitted in this archaeological survey of the monuments of Alexandria.

It appears that it was Cleopatra VII who began its construction, at least in the form of an altar in the middle of a sanctuary intended for the cult of Mark Antony. But the suicide of the Roman general and that of Cleopatra herself in 30 BC, after their defeat at Actium, meant that the queen never completed the project. The victor, Octavian, was determined to erase every memory of Mark Antony and had all his statues knocked down. Although there was originally a large number of them throughout the city, to date only a single one has been found. As for the Caesareum, he decided to complete the building by dedicating it apparently to his own cult. It was clearly a major project, since two obelisks that Pharaoh Tuthmosis III had consecrated fourteen centuries earlier to Re, the Sun god and lord of Heliopolis, were brought from the sanctuary of Heliopolis (which, as we have seen in the case of the blocks of the pharaonic period found on the Pharos site, was by now in ruins and served as a quarry). These two obelisks, which travellers were to dub 'Cleopatra's Needles', marked the entry to the new sanctuary and were to remain there for two millennia, whereas the rest of the temple was to suffer many vicissitudes, especially during the Christian period, before disappearing completely.

The temple

OF THE TEMPLE ITSELF nothing survives beyond descriptions by ancient authors. Its location is certain, however, both because the obelisks stood there until recently and because in 1874 Neroutzos found some massive foundations. Works carried out between the two obelisks and the modern cinema revealed the foundation courses of a wall 3.5 metres (11½ ft) thick; unfortunately, though, we have only a brief description and no drawing. As for the appearance and the dimensions of the sanctuary, we learn about them not from Strabo, who mentions it only briefly, but from Philo of Alexandria (mid-first century AD): 'For there is elsewhere no precinct like that which is called the Sebasteum, a temple to Caesar, patron of sailors, situated on an eminence facing the harbours famed for their excellent moorings, huge and conspicuous […], forming a precinct of vast breadth, embellished with porticoes, libraries, men's banqueting halls, groves, propylaea, spacious courts, open-air

ΕΙΣΕΙΣ
ΕΡΜΗΙΟΕ
ΛΙΒΥ Ϟ ΚΑ
ΚΑΤΤΑ

A little marble plaque with a dedication made to Isis, Sarapis and Hermes by a man called Libys ('the Libyan') together with his wife and children (second century BC). On the left is an ibis clutching a beribboned caduceus in its claws: the ibis is the symbol of the Egyptian god Thoth and the caduceus that of the Greek god Hermes, who has taken the place of Thoth here in the triad he forms with Isis and Osiris. Osiris himself has been replaced by the Alexandrian god Sarapis.

rooms: in short, everything which lavish expenditure could produce to beautify it – the whole a hope of safety to the voyager either going into or out of the harbour.'[28] This description of the architecture of the Caesareum, even though it seems to be giving only a general impression, is one of the most detailed in Alexandrian literature and can be compared only with Rufinus' description of the Sarapeion. Some information can be derived from it about the function and arrangement of the sanctuary in the first century.

The imperial cult

The Caesareum (also referred to as Kaisareion or Sebasteion) was the temple in which the cult of the emperor as the holder of supreme power was practised, the cult of Octavian (Augustus) and his successors. The ruler was honoured here in particular in a role appropriate in a temple beside the sea, as

'Cleopatra's Needles', obelisks originally erected by Pharaoh Tuthmosis III in the temple of Re at Heliopolis and later brought by Augustus to Alexandria to mark the entrance of the Caesareum, the sanctuary dedicated to the imperial cult. These two monuments are the ones most often represented in travellers' drawings. Below: an engraving by David Roberts (1846). Opposite page: an engraving by Fredrick L. Norden (1737).

Excavations in the vicinity of the Caesareum

the protector of sailors or *epibaterios*. It also served as a landmark for seafarers entering the Eastern Harbour (Megas Limen). As Philo wrote, it was 'full of dedicated offerings, covered all around with pictures and statues and objects of silver and of gold', which doubtless included tokens of gratitude from sailors for the deity who had protected them, for example an ex-voto of a captain on an altar found during work on the foundations of the modern synagogue: 'Lucius Tonneius Anteros [has dedicated this altar] to Fair Voyage, for the safety of his ship, *Nikastarte*. In year 43 of Caesar [Augustus], on the twenty-first of Mechir.'

The architecture

Philo's description enables us to imagine the architectural layout of the temple: a huge open court surrounded by stoas that must have served as the outer walls of the sanctuary, just as at the Sarapeion. The rooms in the stoas must have housed books in the much same way as the other libraries in Alexandria; and some of them could have served as assembly rooms. In the open space between the stoas and the temple were the 'sacred groves and the open-air rooms' – but it is difficult to reconstruct the arrangement and function of the latter.

Finally, the temple proper in the centre of the enclosure was presumably built in the Greek style, if one can go by the scanty remains found by Napoleon's scholars. According to Saint-Genis, it would even have been built in the Doric order: 'But one can no longer recognize anything, at any rate not with certainty, of this temple of Caesar. One can however see, a few paces away and also on the seashore, some ruins which form the base of an Arab building and belong to a structure of the Greek or Roman period: one can make out the capitals of some engaged columns which belong to the Doric order. Their shafts rise from the sea-bed. And that is all one can really attribute to the Caesareum.'[29]

IN 1992–3, I CONDUCTED TWO EXCAVATIONS in the vicinity of the Caesareum: one on the site of the former Majestic Cinema, the other on that of the Billiardo Palace. On the first site, a long wall came to light at the bottom of a trial trench. It is constructed of large blocks laid as headers and can be dated by coins to the end of the first century BC. Its orientation is the same as that of the streets running east–west on Mahmud el-Falaki's grid plan (nineteenth century; see pp. 22–3) and it is contemporary with the Caesareum, but it is impossible to say to what part of the sanctuary it could belong. One of the finds at the Billiardo aroused our interest – a column

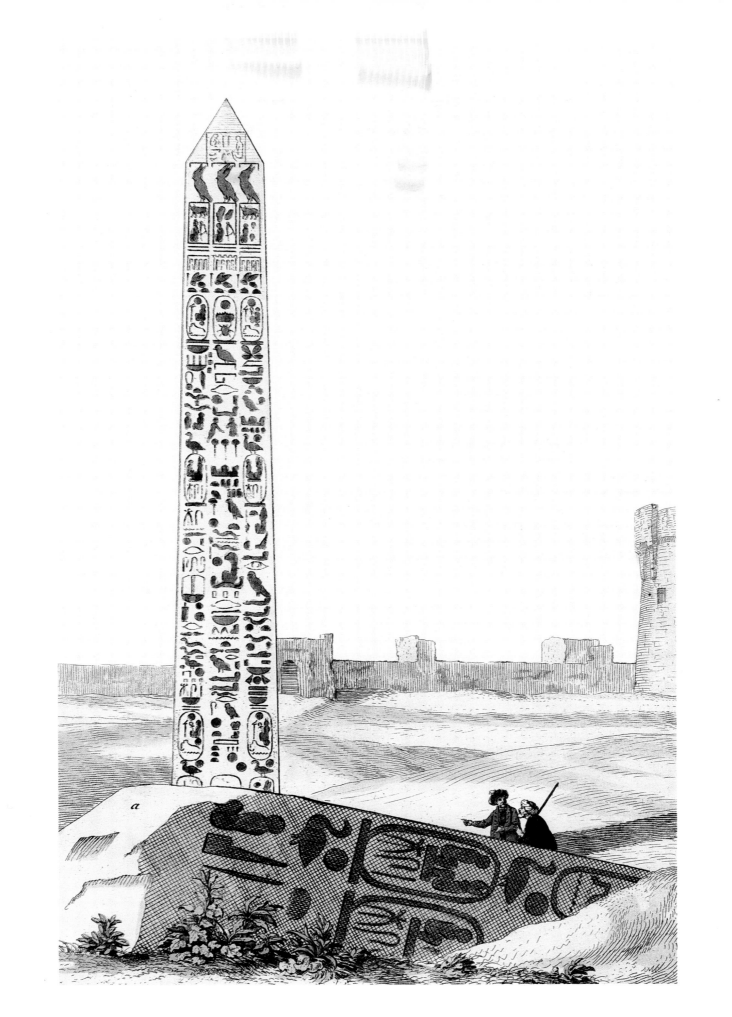

Another view of Cleopatra's Needles. It shows how far the coast has crept inland since antiquity. In the background is the Tower of the Romans, which must be part of the ancient wall incorporated in the ninth-century perimeter.

with a Greek inscription honouring a magistrate (an *epitropos* or Roman procurator) responsible for looking after the images of the emperor – without doubt an important person at the temple. In this temple dedicated to the cult of the imperial family, portrait busts (*imagines* in Latin, *eikones* in Greek) of the different masters of Rome from Augustus (or even Caesar) to Marcus Aurelius were displayed for public veneration and the staff assigned to their service performed sacrifices and other ritual ceremonies. The inscription can be dated to the winter of 175/6, when Marcus Aurelius spent some months in Alexandria.

It mentions the portrait of his wife, Faustina the Younger – who had just died during the voyage – calling her *pharia*. She is thus assimilated to the Isis of the Pharos and must therefore have been depicted like the Isis on the coins struck during this period at the mint in Alexandria, holding a swelling sail (just like her mother, Faustina the Elder, wife of Antoninus Pius, a few years earlier). Faustina is also called *sosistolos*, Saviour of the Fleet: this is a *hapax* (a word found only in this one place, according to the Greek lexicons), but its meaning is clear.

This double epithet, *pharia* and *sosistolos*, is far from surprising in a sanctuary which for two centuries had guaranteed the protection of sailors. When Faustina's death was reported, the Senate had statues erected in her honour at Rome; Marcus Aurelius or the Alexandrians will have done the same in the Caesareum. This event shows that statues of the empresses were placed beside those of the emperors and were associated with them in the imperial cult. Such statues, and possibly also paintings, furnished the temple described by Philo, and they were cared for by the magistrate honoured in the inscription found in our emergency excavations.

These excavations have also brought to light hundreds of coins of the period of the Tetrarchy (293–305). They are a reminder of the fact that, in the course of his monetary reform at the end of the third century, Diocletian installed a mint at Alexandria (the only one in Egypt), in the precinct of the Caesareum. The temple was to retain this function into the fourth century, when the growth of Christianity in the city resulted in the

Christians installing their cathedral in this highly symbolic sanctuary. In the place of the imperial cult, and in the face of bitter pagan resistance, they built a big church there in about 350. Constantius II granted it to the Arian bishop Gregory of Cappadocia (bishop from 339 to 346). It burned down under the Emperor Julian 'the Apostate', and was rebuilt by Athanasius after his death. According to the *History of the Fathers of the Alexandrian Church*, one of the last great representatives of pagan philosophy, Hypatia, was assassinated here in 415 (see p. 96). The final destruction of the sanctuary took place in 912.

Although no certainly identifiable remains of it have ever been found, the Caesareum is none the less one of the few monuments of Alexandria which can be located with some precision: in the area between the place where 'Cleopatra's Needles' once stood and the site of the Billiardo Palace, where our emergency excavation brought to light the inscription mentioned above. Its remains lie under a block of apartment buildings and under the French Market. This latter, which is only a one-storeyed building, is bound to fall prey to property developers in the near future. Let us hope that the archaeologists will be on the spot when that happens, and that they will be allowed the time to uncover the remains of what was for the Alexandrian writer Philo, a sanctuary 'the equal of which does not exist elsewhere'.

THE CAESAREUM, which, as we have seen, was probably built in the Greek style, also had some Egyptianizing features, as is shown by the two obelisks that Augustus had erected in front of the entrance. These obelisks have an unusual history in that they were cut in the granite quarries at Aswan more than a thousand years before Alexandria was founded and, once in front of the Caesareum, remained in place until the nineteenth century, forming a distinctive feature of the landscape long after the temple itself had been destroyed. They were described again and again by travellers, for whom a walk out to see them was a 'must'. The hieroglyphs that cover their surfaces inform us that Tuthmosis III had them erected in front of the Temple of the Sun at Heliopolis in the first half of the fifteenth century BC. Two centuries later, Ramses II indulged in one of his favourite activities, appropriating the monuments of his predecessors, and had his own dedication carved on two sides of Tuthmosis' obelisk. The obelisks remained at Heliopolis nearly one and a half millennia, surviving the great fire which ravaged the sanctuary.

Strabo says that the place was deserted.[30] At Alexandria, plenty of evi-

Cleopatra's Needles

A bronze crab was found at the base of one of Cleopatra's Needles. When the eastern obelisk (the one that had remained upright) was removed, the base was cleared and it became apparent that the monolith was wedged in place with four bronze crabs, one of which had escaped the notice of robbers. It bears an inscription which allows us to date the transport of the stone to 13 BC.

dence has been found of the Ptolemies' and the Romans' habit of 'borrowing' from the sanctuary, which they treated like a huge quarry. Our underwater excavations at the site of the Pharos have shown that sphinxes, obelisks, papyrus columns and other items of pharaonic architecture were transported to Alexandria and gave the Ptolemies' capital an 'Egyptian look'.[31] In 13 BC, Augustus had Tuthmosis' two obelisks brought to Alexandria to be erected in front of the brand-new Caesareum. We know this from a bilingual inscription in Greek and Latin, carved on a bronze crab preserved in the Metropolitan Museum of Art in New York: 'In year 18 of Caesar [Augustus], Barbarus, Prefect of Egypt, dedicated [this obelisk]; the architect was Pontius.'

This crab was one of the bronze crustaceans that served as wedges under the obelisks. They are mentioned by Yakubi of Baghdad, who spent some time as an official in Egypt. In 870 he expressed his admiration for 'Alexandria, a great and splendid city of indescribable size and beauty'. After a long account of the Pharos, he notes, 'there are also two obelisks in variegated stone, resting on crayfish of copper and covered in ancient inscriptions.' Originally there were eight crabs, all probably with the same inscription. Seven of them were removed over the years, presumably for their valuable metal. Moving the obelisks was not an easy task: they are 20.87 and 21.2 metres (68½ and 69 ft) high respectively, and weigh 186 and 200 tons. Although Pontius is named as the architect who directed the operation, we do not know whether the transport was the work of Egyptians who had kept their traditional skills or of Alexandrian engineers. We possess a number of treatises on applied mechanics from this period. Heron of Alexandria (first century AD?), the brilliant successor of the Ptolemaic mechanists, explains how many hoists and how many men are necessary to raise a given weight to a given height. Pliny the Elder, author of a catalogue of the obelisks erected at Alexandria, relates how Ptolemy II Philadelphus 'borrowed' an obelisk from Heliopolis in the mid-third century BC, to transport it to the building-site of the Arsinoeion. He describes how the obelisk was floated down the Nile and how it was erected, and also says that the Prefect of Egypt, Maximus, had it removed to the nearby forum because it was obstructing the dockyards. This obelisk was brought to Rome by Caligula and now stands in St Peter's Square.

WRITING AT THE END OF THE NINTH CENTURY, Yakubi mentions two obelisks, as do Idrissi in 1154 and Abd el-Latif of Baghdad in 1200.[32] The westerly one seems to have fallen over after Abdel Latif's visit, probably in 1303, following one of the violent earthquakes that contributed to the destruction of the Pharos. The maritime map in Montpellier has a note beside the position of Alexandria: '8 August 1303: collapse of the Pharos.' As we saw in connection with the destruction of the Pharos, there was an increase in tectonic activity in the region in the first half of the fourteenth century (remember that Ibn Battuta visited the first storey of the Pharos during his first stay in 1329, but was unable to get to it in 1346). It is likely that the western obelisk fell around this time. An engraving made by André Thévet in 1550 shows only one still standing.

The obelisks of the Caesareum are now commonly known as 'Cleopatra's Needles', recalling the tendency of latter-day travellers to attribute ancient remains to Egypt's last queen.[33] However, they have had various names over the centuries: some travellers connected them with 'Pharaoh', and others even with Virgil! The Englishman George Sandys wrote in 1611: 'Of Antiquities, there are few remainders; onely an Hieroglyphical Obelisk of *Theban* marble, as hard well-nigh as Porphyries, but of a deeper red, and speckled alike, called *Pharaoh's Needle*, standing where once stood the palace of *Alexander:* and another lying by, and like it, half buryed in rubbidge.'

It appears that Sandys was drawing on an account by John Evesham (1586) and that he in his turn influenced an anonymous Scot who passed through Alexandria in 1656. In fact, only English-speaking travellers speak of 'Pharaoh's Needle'. The Abbé Binos, who visited Alexandria in 1777, saw the famous 'needles' too, but his guide gave them a different name: 'among the ancient monuments still standing he mentions the obelisk of Virgil, which is near the sumptuous palace of Armida, [...] of which Tasso has spoken.' That this is not made up is shown by the fact that more than two centuries earlier, in 1533, Greffin Affagart, a rich nobleman from the Maine region of France, recorded the existence of this obelisk, a stone 'higher and thicker than the one at Rome which they call "Vergil's [bone] splinter"'. In 1550 Thévet produced his engraving of 'Cleopatra's Needle', as we have seen, and it was this name that carried the day. As the centuries passed, it was adopted by all travellers and translated into practically every language. In 1877, it was realized that the obelisks had been erected after Cleopatra's death, that she had not seen them at Alexandria and, moreover, that Strabo has nothing to say about them because they were brought to Alexandria in 13 BC, seventeen years after the death of the last of the Ptolemies.

The Needles in the modern period

This engraving shows the scenes carved on the pedestal of another obelisk of Pharaoh Tuthmosis III, which was brought to the hippodrome at Byzantium. It can still be viewed today at Istanbul, not far from Hagia Sophia. The obelisk was dragged by means of pulleys. This gearing-down of forces demonstrates the technique explained by the Alexandrian engineers whose treatises have survived. It differs in this respect from the practice of the ancient Egyptians, as illustrated in bas-reliefs.

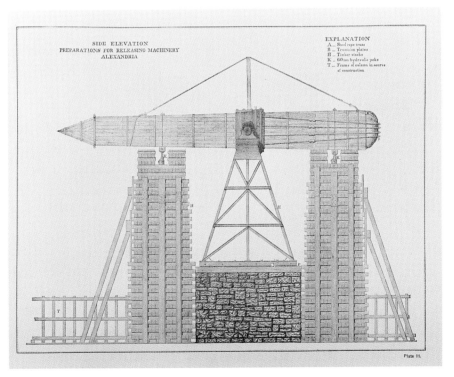

SIDE ELEVATION
PREPARATIONS FOR RELEASING MACHINERY
ALEXANDRIA

EXPLANATION
A — Steel rope truss
B — Trunnion plates
H — Timber stacks
K — 60 ton hydraulic jacks
T — Frame of caisson in course
of construction

Plate III.

The fallen obelisk lay undisturbed until 1877. However, it was not entirely unaffected by the frenzy which took hold of the city as a result of the development encouraged by Mohammed Ali from the 1820s onwards. Its base, a block of Aswan granite weighing around forty tons, was blown up by engineers to provide stone for neighbouring building sites.

The English had been on the point of carrying it off in 1801. Besides the antiquities confiscated from the French after Menou's capitulation (which included the Rosetta stone), Lord Cavan, the commander of the ground forces, wanted to carry off a trophy as a memorial to the glory of Admiral Nelson and of General Abercromby, who had lost his life in the victorious battle against the French on the plain of Abukir. Getting the consent of the Turks had been no more than a formality, and the troops had clubbed together for the removal of the trophy. A stone jetty had been constructed and a boat found, when the order came from the Admiralty to attend to more urgent matters.

The gift of the monument to England was confirmed by Mohammed Ali in 1819, and again in 1831, but as funds were not forthcoming, it remained in Alexandria. Although France had already moved one of the obelisks from Luxor, which Mohammed Ali had offered, to the Place de la Concorde in 1836, it was only at the end of the century that a rich doctor, Erasmus Wilson, undertook the removal of the fallen obelisk at his own expense.

After some oriental-style haggling with the Greek owner of the land on which it lay (he expected compensation), the engineer John Dixon, a pupil of George Stephenson, clothed the obelisk in a cylinder of steel, which was soon afloat in the Eastern Harbour. This strange contraption, which was suitably baptized *Cleopatra*, was then towed by a boat towards the open sea. Unfortunately, a storm got up in the Bay of Biscay; the tow-rope broke and six men lost their lives. The obelisk drifted for several days before being found and rescued by another English ship, which was cruising in these waters. Its owner, however, regarded the obelisk as salvage and demanded that it be bought back from him – and that is what was done. When the weather turned fair again, the *Cleopatra* was towed without further mishap into the Thames. After much discussion as to where it should stand – in front of Westminster Abbey, the Houses of Parliament or the British Museum – Cleopatra's Needle was finally erected on the north bank of the Thames, where it can be admired today, despite German air raids in the two world wars (the raid on 4 September 1917 was nearly fatal: part of the pedestal was blown away).

The removal of the other obelisk to New York was less eventful but

OPPOSITE PAGE, TOP: The London obelisk. During transport it was placed in a specially constructed boat, the *Cleopatra*, and towed as far as the Bay of Biscay. A storm took the sailors by surprise and six of them were drowned. The *Cleopatra* drifted until it was recovered by another English vessel.

BELOW: The Alexandrian obelisk in the London sunshine. Its worn base has been encased in a bronze cladding decorated with Egyptian motifs.

OPPOSITE PAGE, BOTTOM: The New York obelisk. Left: The eastern obelisk shortly before its departure. Right: A scaffold with a central pivot was constructed to erect one of Cleopatra's Needles in Central Park, New York, in 1880.

The eastern obelisk was offered to the Americans, who removed it in 1879. The operation was photographed: here the American flag is to be seen flying at the top of the monument. This demonstration of ownership was provoked by the opposition of a large number of Egyptians to the obelisk's departure. Captain Gorringe had learned from the British experience, and chose a different method of transporting it overseas: he bought an old Egyptian ship and opened the bows to slide in the obelisk. The Alexandrian obelisk was erected in Central Park in front of a crowd of curious onlookers.

equally spectacular. The Americans' interest in the acquisition of such a monument was principally fuelled by the example of the French and the British. As in the case of Britain, the costs of the operation were met by a private individual, William Vanderbilt, who had made his fortune on the railways. The negotiations were conducted with the Khedive Ismaïl. In spite of opposition both in the United States and in Egypt, where people were upset to see their country dispossessing itself of yet another of its treasures, the operation began in 1879. Captain Gorringe, who was in charge of the manoeuvre, has left an excellent book on the different phases of the undertaking with a series of spectacular photographs. They reveal how, in order to ward off any attempt on the part of the local population to reclaim the obelisk, the American flag was promptly run up above the pyramidion; and how, with the help of a steel device, the obelisk was lowered and transported by sea to the Western Harbour, where it was slid into a freighter from which a portion of the hull had been removed. At New York, the overland transport was effected by means of railtracks laid right up to the place where it was to be erected. In 1881, a steel gantry crane was used to re-erect the obelisk, in a manner both simple and spectacular, on its original pedestal in the middle of Central Park, near the Metropolitan Museum of Art.

Today only engravings and old maps show us where Cleopatra's Needles once stood. People lost no time in erecting buildings in their place: do the guests of the Hotel Metropole realize, I wonder, that they are sleeping on the spot where almost two millennia ago the monumental entrance markers of the Caesareum stood?

CHAPTER SEVEN

A city
of cisterns

OPPOSITE: The
cistern of el-Nabih,
the only one now
open to the public.
It is composed
of a three-storey
colonnade in
sixteen rows.

A cistern at Alexandria
(reconstruction
drawing by an
architect employed by
the Graeco-Roman
Museum, around
1915).

WHEN I ARRIVED IN ALEXANDRIA IN 1990, only one ancient cistern could be visited. It was the only one the inhabitants could remember. What a loss of memory, considering that the scholars who accompanied Napoleon had counted more than four hundred, and that a few decades later Mahmud el-Falaki had listed seven hundred! Even this number was modest compared to the estimate of the English traveller Henry Blunt, who had visited Alexandria in 1634 and noted that: 'Fresh water is brought to Alexandria in a large, and deepe channell cut by men, almost fourscore miles, through the wildernesse to the Nile … It is conveighed and kept in *Cisternes*, whereof there remain but five hundred, of two thousand at the first.' This memory loss is puzzling; how is one to account for the disappearance from the map, in less than a century, of so many monuments that various descriptions represent as veritable subterranean cathedrals?

Between 1710 and 1712 François Paumier, a member of the third order of St Francis, exclaimed with admiration: 'there is nothing more beautiful and complete than the vaults; nothing better constructed than their apertures; nothing more superb than the pieces of marble with which they are surrounded.' Numerous engravings of the seventeenth and eighteenth centuries give us an idea of the imposing proportions of the cisterns, and the *Description de l'Egypte* devotes several plates to them. The English periodical *The Graphic*, in a report on the events of 1882 (the shelling of the city centre by the British Navy), gives an illustrated account of intrepid visitors armed with hurricane lamps, venturing on the exploration of these huge subterranean spaces. We see them balancing precariously on the arches which link the rows of columns rising out of depths shrouded in darkness.

Alexandria was a city of cisterns, like Constantinople. Nowadays in Istanbul visitors can walk about in these huge halls of columns stretching away endlessly. In one of the biggest, the Basilica (Yerebatan), planks of wood have been laid just above the stagnant water for the convenience of visitors, and it is a breathtaking experience to find oneself confronted with the long rows of cunningly illuminated columns and their reflections in the water, or when one suddenly comes face to face with a huge marble Medusa with her petrifying gaze, placed the wrong way up to support a column.

The large number of cisterns in Alexandria astonished Napoleon's scholars during the years they spent in the city (1798–1801), and (somewhat later) Mahmud el-Falaki. As we have seen, Khedive Ismaïl had instructed el-Falaki to draw up a plan of the ancient city. In his book, published in 1872, el-Falaki explained that Alexandria was 'superimposed on another city of

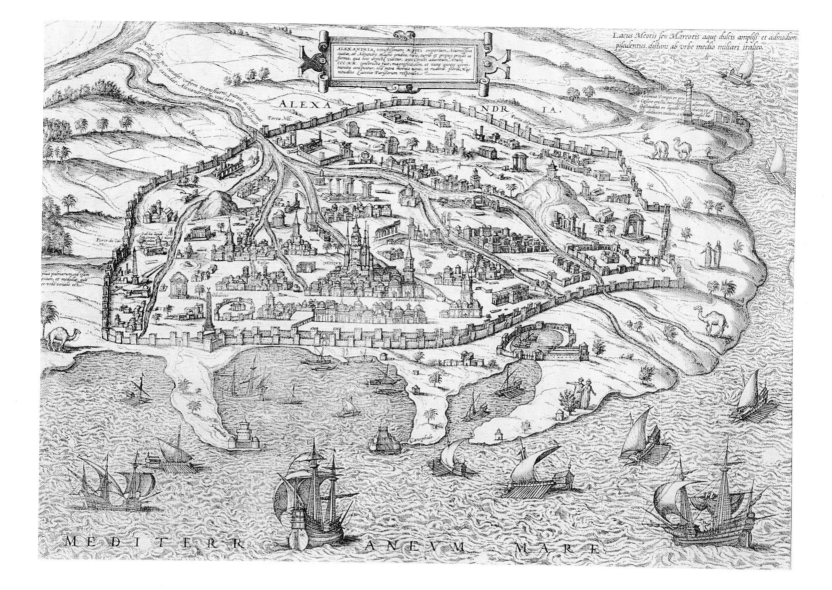

cisterns, the streets of which are subterranean canals'. But by the time I arrived, all trace of this underground city had disappeared. Just one cistern was still to be seen, that of el-Nabih. Its beauty and its huge proportions only made the loss of the others even more regrettable.

HYDRAULICS WAS A CONTINUAL OBSESSION of the Alexandrians and their successive overlords; the development of the city had always been dependent on the quality of its water. In his *Alexandrian War*,[34] Caesar relates how, after he had fortified the great theatre and entrenched himself there, he experienced an unexpected difficulty: the Alexandrians had made the wells he depended on unusable by contaminating them with sea water:

This view of Alexandria in the seventeenth century shows the branches of the Canopic canal supplying the different quarters of the city with water (Jansson's *Atlas*, 1619).

The city water supply

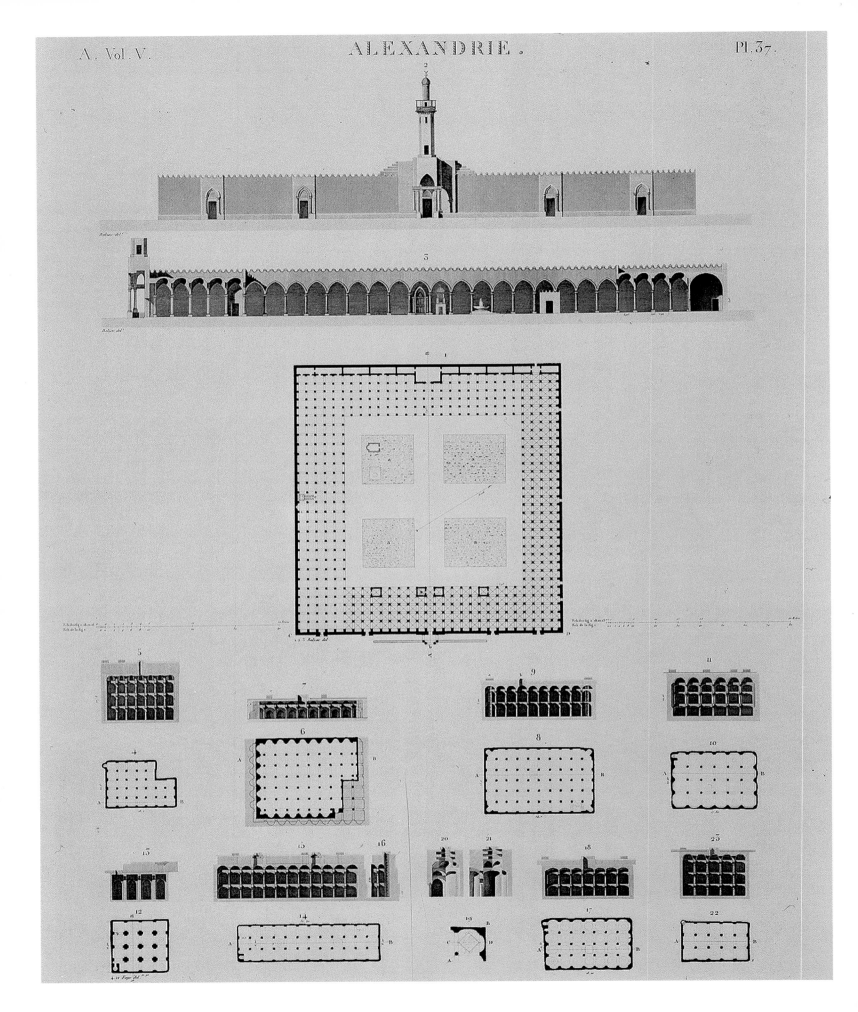

'Soon the water drawn from the houses nearest [to the enemy] was a little more brackish than usual, and occasioned no little wonder among the men as to why this had come about. Nor could they quite believe the evidence of their own ears when their neighbours lower down said that the water they were using was of the same kind and taste as they had previously been accustomed to; and they were openly discussing the matter among themselves and, by tasting samples, learning how markedly the waters differed. However, in a short space of time the water nearer the contamination was

OPPOSITE PAGE: Plate from the *Description de l'Egypte*, with ground plans and section drawings of cisterns recorded by the scholars of the Napoleonic expedition.

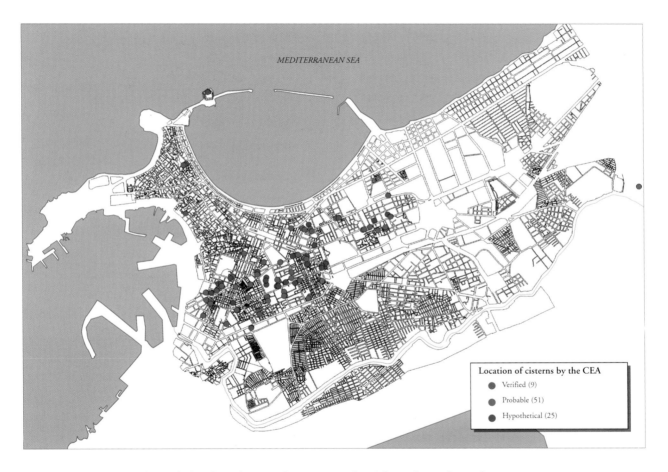

MEDITERRANEAN SEA

Location of cisterns by the CEA
Verified (9)
Probable (51)
Hypothetical (25)

entirely undrinkable, while that lower down was found to be relatively impure and brackish. This circumstance dispelled their doubts, and so great was the panic that took hold upon them that it seemed that they were all reduced to a most hazardous plight, and some asserted that Caesar was being slow in giving orders to embark.'[35]

In danger of being forced to give in, Caesar had to find a speedy solution: he had wells sunk down to the water-table and was thus able cleverly to redress a situation which was becoming critical. It is important to remember

Plan of the modern city showing the cisterns located by Isabelle Hairy and Yves Guyard.

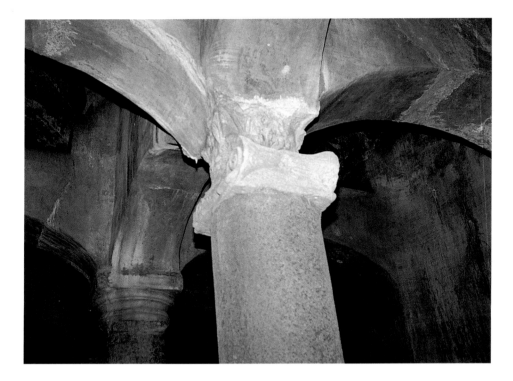

Column shafts and ancient capitals were often reused in the Alexandrian cisterns. In the cistern of el-Nabih (opposite page), a strange combination can be seen: a Corinthian capital resting directly on an octagonal base.

that, as this passage from Caesar shows, the cisterns of Alexandria were linked by the system of conduits which fed them, which meant that they could easily be poisoned; also that the quality of the water in them could have dire consequences: Caesar nearly lost the war he was waging against the Alexandrians because he had no control over it.

During the winter months – especially January and February – it rains at irregular intervals in Alexandria, but, with the exception of the three centuries of Ottoman occupation (1517–1805), the Alexandrians have never regarded these random rainfalls as an essential source of water. From the city's earliest history, they have preferred to rely on a twenty-kilometre-long canal (12 miles), dug from the Canopic branch of the Nile, to ensure a regular and controlled supply.

Various accounts by travellers over the preceding centuries enable us to follow the progress of the water from the Nile into the canal and then into the subsidiary channels which brought it into the city and its intercommunicating cisterns.

The canal

THIS CANAL PLAYED A VITAL ROLE in the city's history, and its maintenance was a perpetual concern not only of the Ptolemies, but of the Romans and the Muslim dynasties as well. We have a number of lapidary inscriptions and literary texts which mention cleaning, widenings and

repairs. For instance, a bilingual inscription, in Greek and Latin, found near the Canopic Gate, states that Augustus renovated the canal in AD 10–11: 'The emperor Caesar, son of a god, Augustus, high priest, has brought the august river to Schedia, so that it flows […] through the whole city. [Given] when Gaius Julius Aquila was prefect of Egypt, in the year 40 of Caesar.'

The archaeological remains and above all the accounts of travellers, both Arab and Western, provide us with information about this reliance on the waters of the Nile. A special feature of Alexandria that must be emphasized is that, in contrast to the rest of the Greek world, in the dry season the rising of the Nile used to bring the city more water than usual. The water supply had to be regulated by means of dams and locks. In 1318 Abul Feda, Prince of Hama and a relative of the Ayyubids, went into raptures: 'the canal, which comes from the Nile, is an enchanting sight. It is steep-sided, covered in greenery on both banks and surrounded by gardens. The poet Dhafer, also called Alhaddad, praises it too: "how often has it offered to your eyes in the evening light a sight which filled your heart with the purest of delight!"'

In 1422, Ghillebert de Lannoy,[36] who had been instructed by Henry V of England to report to him on the state of the region in connection with a plan to re-establish a Christian kingdom in Jerusalem, gave this description: 'Underneath the streets and houses, the whole city is hollow. Under the ground there are conduits roofed over with arches, through which the wells are filled up once a year by the River Nile. And if this were not so, they would have no fresh water in the town, since it rains there very little or not at all and there are neither wells nor natural springs in the city. Thirty miles from here, starting from a village on the Nile called Hatse, a man-made canal begins its course. It runs for a mile close to the city, along the walls, and flows into the sea in the Old Harbour [Western Harbour]. Every year, at the end of August and throughout all of September, the River Nile, which rises considerably at this time of year, flows through this canal to fill all the wells of the city for a year, and also the wells outside the city, which are used for watering the gardens.'

In 1737, Captain Norden of the Danish Royal Navy speaks in his turn of the canal which he calls 'the *calisch* or canal of Cleopatra' (*calisch* is a deformation of *khalig* – the Arabic for canal – and it is attributed to Cleopatra, like all things ancient): 'It was simply dug out of the earth, without being re-inforced by any facing in stone or brick and it has filled up by degrees.[…] Nowadays it resembles a badly maintained ditch, and only just enough water flows in it to fill the reservoirs required to meet the needs of modern Alexandria. I crossed it dry-shod in the month of June.'[37]

To sum up, from the principal canal running from east to west, several subsidiary, underground canals branched off to run from south to north and feed the cisterns of the old city within the walls, but not the Ottoman town. In the eighteenth century, the former was nothing more than ruins covered in gardens. The small cisterns which had been installed there near houses and mosques were fed by rainwater and by what could be drawn from the large cisterns of the ancient city, as the archimandrite Constantine of Kiev recalled in 1795: 'For these cisterns [those of the Graeco-Roman city] are only reservoirs of water, which [store it, but] do not cleanse it. To draw it out, water pumps are used, by means of which the water is poured into leather bags specially made for this purpose. These are brought by camel or by ass to New Alexandria [the Ottoman city], where the water is sold.'

The press has taken an interest in Alexandria since the British bombardment in 1882. Here, an article in the London periodical *The Graphic* shows visitors in one of the city's ancient cisterns still in use at that time.

For several centuries, it was possible to trace the course of an underground canal running south-north thanks to some holes still visible on the surface, as Norden notes in 1737: 'However, one can see a walled place there – this is where the aqueduct starts which one can follow right over the plain, and even as far as Alexandria; for, although it is under the ground, the ventilation holes which exist at intervals help us to trace accurately enough the route it takes to reach the reservoirs or cisterns, which are found only in what we have seen to be the ancient city.'

A series of these holes figures on the plan drawn up by Napoleon's scholars. Ghillebert de Lannoy also recorded the existence of an iron grating at the point at which the south–north canals branch off the main canal: 'And in the

south-west, a mile from the aforementioned river, there is an iron grating in the ditch where the conduits start which carry the water into the city.'[38] This description of 1422 may be compared with that of Emmanuel Piloti two years earlier: 'The city of Alexandria is situated in a waterless place, and only has wells of brackish water. But each house is built above an underground chamber, in which there is a cistern which fills with water. Thus, every year after the Nile flood, thanks to the man-made ditch described above – this ditch is called *caliz* – by which the waters reach the walls of Alexandria, there is a passage where there is an opening with an iron grating, and the waters enter through the conduits into the wells of the city.' Clearly, the grating was there to stop intruders from taking the city via the underground aqueducts.

During the Second World War, several ancient cisterns were converted into air-raid shelters. They were provided with concrete floors, brick partition walls, benches, and sometimes even pumped air.

The Mahmudiya Canal in 1910. It was dug in 1829 on Mohammed Ali's orders and followed the course of the ancient canal for a considerable distance. In 1910 the area surrounding it was still a pleasant place for an outing – one of these spots was even called the 'Champs-Elysées'. Nowadays, this derelict canal has become a sewer.

OPPOSITE PAGE: Perspective view of the el-Nabih cistern with its arched arcades. It almost certainly dates from the ninth century AD.

The water brought by the Nile flood was full of silt and obviously unfit for drinking. Travellers relate how people waited patiently for the water to clear, in the meantime drinking that which had been kept from the year before. 'The water in the cisterns', writes Villamont in 1590, 'in which it has recently arrived, is very bad to drink, causing fever and dysentery, which usually kill those affected. Accordingly, the inhabitants who are careful about their health, keep the water from the year before to use until November.'

Almost a century later, in 1672, Father Vansleb, who was sent to Egypt by Colbert to buy papyri, describes the stratagems used to limit the amount of silt and impurities flowing in: the outlet into the main south–north channel which fed the cisterns inside the old city was blocked up and three days were allowed to pass, during which most of the impurities flowed into the sea; then it was opened again with great ceremony: 'There is outside the Rosetta Gate [a canal running south–north]. It is the height of a man and vaulted inside. At a quarter of a league from the town, it meets the *calitz* of Cleopatra,[39] which comes past there and feeds into it some of the water it receives from the Nile

A reused Corinthian capital in the el-Nabih cistern.

itself, before then conveying the water as far as the walls, where, having met another conduit, which is not very far from this gate and which by means of an ingenious system communicates with all the cisterns, it fills them. You must however know that its mouth, although it is as high as the rest of the canal['s tunnel], has almost two thirds of its opening walled up, from bottom to top, so that only a little aperture is left, through which the waters of the *calitz* enter, as if through a window. But because they are very dirty for the first three days, and because the cisterns would soon be filled with dirt if the water were allowed to enter freely during that time, those who are in charge of the town's water supply in order to avoid this inconvenience, immediately have the aperture of this canal walled up and leave it in this state for three days, after which they go to the mouth of the canal, accompanied by a crowd of people to unblock it and allow the water to enter until the cisterns are full. The day of this opening is one of great rejoicing for the whole town.'

As on the occasion of the famous ceremony of the opening of the *khalig* (the aqueduct that brought the water from the Nile to the citadel) at Cairo, that of the canal at Alexandria was celebrated by the population, even though they had to wait before drinking the water if they did not want to become gravely ill.

We have already learned from Father Vansleb of the precautions taken at the end of the seventeenth century. A century earlier, in 1598, Krystof Harant, a Czech nobleman in the service of Emperor Rudolf II, criticized the shortcomings that could lead to serious contamination: 'But as the water arrives there full of mud and as all the mud settles on the floor of the cellar', it caused nauseating smells and an unhealthy atmosphere. 'Moreover, it finally grows stagnant and stinks; and yet people do not cleanse the cellars of the mud and the rubbish before filling them up again. The fresh water is contaminated by the bad water and carries the contagion into the bloodstream of the people, who for this reason suffer, mainly from high fever, which befalls primarily those who cannot stop themselves eating the delicious, fresh fruit which grows there.'

In 1652, Jean de Thévenot has the same story to tell: 'But in the months of August and September, which is when the cisterns are filled, this new water is unhealthy. Few of those who drink it escape getting some illness.' Before the canal was dug, life must have been difficult on the site of the future Alexandria. The fishing village which is believed to have existed there before the foundation of the city must have had problems obtaining fresh water, just as was the case during the Ottoman period, as all the travellers from the West who passed through the city emphasize.

From the fourteenth century, for a hundred years before the Ottoman

invasion, the maintenance of the canal could no longer be taken for granted. Alexandria declined rapidly to the advantage of Rosetta and Dami-etta, its two rivals, situated to the east, on the main branches of the Nile. The Canopic branch, which fed the Alexandrian canal, had rapidly silted up. When Mohammed Ali put the canal back into service, he was obliged to extend it eastwards by about fifty kilometres (30 miles) to the Bolbitine branch of the Nile, which flows into the sea near Rosetta.

The water was drawn from the cisterns with the aid of *saqiehs* – wheels with jars on them. Thévenot describes these machines as follows: 'These lifting devices consist of a wheel with a loop of rope to which are attached at intervals several clay pots (like a rosary); these rise full of water and pour it into a channel which brings it wherever it is wanted.'

Access to the cisterns for cleaning was by well-shafts, as Richard Pococke explains in his account of 1737: 'The cisterns also must be cleansed; and the descent down to them is by round wells, in which there are holes on each side, at about two feet distance, to put the feet in to descend by.'

THIS UNIQUE SURVIVOR among the cisterns of Alexandria, situated in Sharia Sultan Husayn, 200 metres (220 yds) north of the main artery of the ancient city (the Canopic Street), is very impressive. To reach it, one descends a flight of steps to a window which offers a dramatic view into the depths over three storeys of ancient columns. Four rows of columns linked by delicate arches – making a total of forty-eight columns – subdivide a huge space, endowing it with harmonious proportions and lines of perspective receding into the shadows which call to mind certain of Piranesi's engravings. One can recognize shafts of ancient columns there – mainly of Aswan granite – resting on reused elements; finely carved capitals serve as bases, whereas Ionic bases of white marble have been used as capitals. It is a real architectural muddle, with capitals of all shapes, especially Corinthian capitals of the Roman period with finely chiselled acanthus leaves made of marble from the Princes' Islands. Here Constantine of Kiev's description (1795) must be quoted, as it fits this building so exactly that one could swear he had visited it: 'The diversity of the columns which hold up the vaults above the cisterns, the Gothic or Saracen style which one observes in their disposition prove that they are not [now] in their original state; but, as has been said above, on the subject of [the city of] Alexandria in general, when [the columns] were destroyed and when necessity demanded that some of them should be reconstructed, people reassembled them from the collection of parts and fragments [which was left], without bothering to

The cistern of el-Nabih

OVERLEAF: One of the storeys of the el-Nabih cistern, showing the reuse of ancient elements – capitals used as bases and column bases serving as capitals.

recreate them in the form in which they previously existed.' Constantine is actually describing another, relatively recent cistern (which can be dated to the Islamic period) situated at the foot of the city wall built (or at least started) by Ibn Tulun at the end of the ninth century.

Six other cisterns

BY DINT OF INCREASING MY OUTPUT of lectures and articles on the subject, I managed to provoke some reactions from the inhabitants of Alexandria. Bernard de Zogheb started telling me how, during the Second

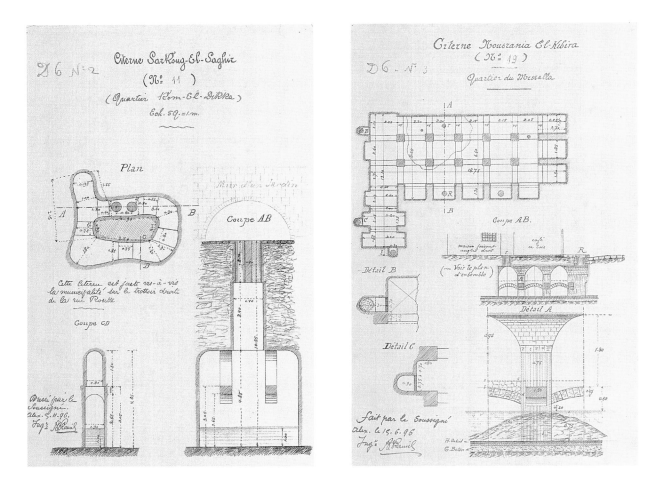

World War, he used to take refuge in a certain cistern in Fuad Street, which served as an air-raid shelter. He told me that people dreaded the German air raids when the guns were rumbling during the gigantic battle of el-Alamein, which was raging less than a hundred kilometres (60 miles) away to the west. The Alexandrians had become accustomed to recognizing the noise made by the engines of the Stukas and used to go down to shelter in the ancient cisterns, which had been converted in a hurry by the authori-

ties of the British occupation force. On the other hand, when they heard the more rapid and lighter throbbing of the Italian planes, they could stake a wager on their missing their targets (which is why the air raids of Mussolini's airforce caused hundreds of casualties, whereas there were relatively few after Nazi raids).

This trail proved a fruitful one, as it enabled me to locate another cistern at the corner of Fuad Street and the Street of the Ptolemies. With the help of the city's Director of Islamic Antiquities, Mohammed Abdel Aziz, we were able to lift two slabs of modern concrete in a cul-de-sac between two early twentieth-century buildings. Steps descended to a first basement fitted out as a shelter, where some partitions made of modern bricks covered with whitewash filled the spaces between columns surmounted by ancient capitals. A concrete floor separated this level from a lower floor reached by a modern flight of steps, but the ground water barred our way, preventing us from going further. We were immediately below the Canopic Street, under which a large conduit had been installed, which obviously fed this cistern. People used to say that an enormous subterranean canal ran from the Gate of the Sun in the east to the Gate of the Moon five kilometres (3 miles) to the west, and that it was so big that a man could sit on a horse in it. Obviously, this water main fed the cisterns along its course, like the one we were looking at.

We made rapid progress when, a little later, Mohammed Abdel Aziz took me to see two other cisterns (which had also served as air-raid shelters), much further to the west; one beside Dar Ismaïl hospital, the other near Kom el-Nadura, at a place called El-Battuta. Again we were confronted with the same partitions of whitewashed brick.

It seemed to us archaeologists that we had struck a rich seam and that the solution was easy: all we had to do to find the cisterns which were converted into air-raid shelters during the Second World War was to find the files – which surely must exist – concerning these relatively recent alterations. Unfortunately, all our efforts, both with the civic administration in Alexandria and in London at the Colonial Office, to gain access to such archives have been in vain.

I was told about other cisterns, for example the one in Sesostris Street, in the middle of the city, but I could not gain access to it, as a shop had been built above its entrance. The shopkeepers themselves confirmed the existence of the cistern – which, according to them, was huge – but it was impossible to get into it. Then I had more luck, and was able to visit a beautiful, harmoniously proportioned cistern nearby, in the courtyard of

the Coptic Orthodox Patriarchate. And I was taken to see a third in the Antoniadis Gardens, three kilometres south-east of the city centre, not far from the airport.

With these ten new cisterns, I felt we had made real progress. These discoveries proved to us that we could hope to locate still more. But we needed to find a method, an Ariadne's thread, that would help us unravel the puzzle. For several years, we were unable to get any further.

The files of the water board and other archives

WE WERE ABLE TO FIND OUR WAY OUT of this impasse thanks to an unexpected discovery. One day, the management of the Graeco-Roman Museum sent us a bundle of documents which had lain undisturbed there for decades. They turned out to be dossiers concerning no less than 140 cisterns in the city! Plans, section drawings and sketches of their locations, drawn up by the municipal water board at the end of the nineteenth century, were accompanied by a list of expenses incurred for repairs. A civil engineer named Kamil had put these dossiers together and included an account of the maintenance and repair of the cisterns, which could be used in a case of need as reservoirs of clean water. Scourges like the plague and cholera had remained endemic at Alexandria, with Lake Mariut serving as a potential source of contagion, and the commerce of the sea-port meant that there was also a considerable danger of epidemics spreading on a scale far beyond the environs of the city (recent studies have shown that the famous plague of Marseille in 1720 definitely came from Alexandria).[40]

Another source came to light shortly afterwards at the Jesuit College in Cairo. Thanks to its librarian, Father Martin, we became aware of a second list of Alexandrian cisterns, drawn up by Galice Bey[41] in 1849, half a century before the water board's inventory. The documents in Cairo, however, were briefer and more difficult to use than Kamil's.

A lot of work remained to be done. It was undertaken by the architect Jean-Luc Arnaud, who set out to search for the cisterns on the ground, armed with the location sketches from the water board dossier. He had soon tracked down more than twenty-five. The ground had been prepared and now it was necessary to assemble a team to develop the study in a systematic manner. Isabelle Hairy and Yves Guyard – both architects – have started pursuing two different lines of research.[42] First, they have completed detailed plans of the layout of some of the cisterns, for example, a section drawing of the cistern of el-Nabih and drawings of its forty-eight capitals. This work will serve as the basis for the restoration, improvement and presentation to the public of the best-preserved of Alexandria's cisterns, following the

example of what has been done with the cisterns at Istanbul. It may be hoped that this major project will be rewarded with success in a few years' time and will reopen a group of undeservedly forgotten monuments to the Alexandrians and their visitors.

The second part of this research project is to try to locate the other cisterns mentioned in the museum's dossier. So far, almost a hundred have been identified on the ground. This rediscovery is indicative of the cyclical nature of Alexandrian history. After having become within only a few generations the capital of the Hellenistic world, by the Ottoman period it was a village, before again becoming, in the nineteenth century, one of the major cities of the Mediterranean. Investigations are continuing to make good progress. Some new cisterns have been found in the district adjoining the ancient Heptastadion, and another beside Qait Bey Fort.[43] Not a month passes without our being informed of another one to add to our list. Through them the whole history of hydraulic engineering and construction at Alexandria is coming to light.

Plans, sections and sketches by the engineer Kamil, indicating the location of two other ancient cisterns. The archives of the Graeco-Roman Museum contain documentation on 140 cisterns, a good number of which have successfully been located.

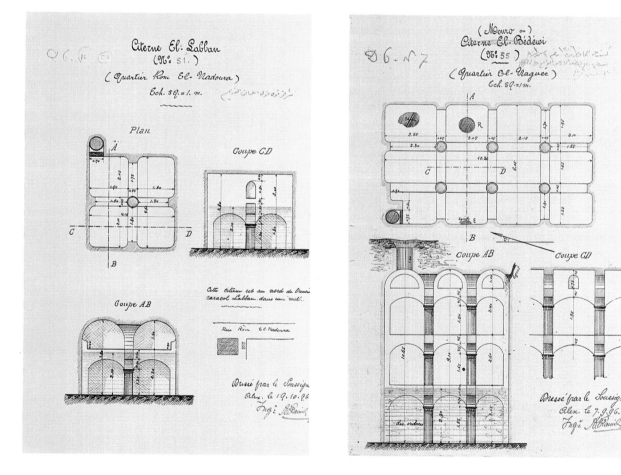

CHAPTER EIGHT

In search of Alexander's tomb

OPPOSITE: The Alabaster Tomb in the Latin cemetery. As Adriani has shown, it is the antechamber of a large subterranean funerary monument, like the royal hypogea discovered in Macedonia. It has been dated to the early third century BC, and both its date and its luxuriousness prompted Adriani to suggest that it might be the tomb of Alexander. Even if this is not the case, it must surely be the resting place of a high dignitary of the Ptolemaic kingdom.

The epic story of Alexander and the search for his tomb have been recurrent themes in the Western imagination. Here, a detail of a fifteenth-century miniature from a copy of the *History of Alexander* written by the Latin historian Quintus Curtius in the first century AD shows the monks burying Alexander. Bibliothèque Municipale, Reims.

OPPOSITE PAGE: Two views of the interior of the Alabaster Tomb. The upper photograph gives an idea of the unusual thickness of the slabs of alabaster quarried in the mountains of Upper Egypt. The lower photograph shows how the veining of this beautiful substance forms a natural decoration. The doorway in the background used to lead to another, lower, chamber of the tomb, which has now disappeared without trace.

WHY ON EARTH DO PEOPLE PERSIST in searching for *the* tomb of Alexander, when there were actually several? It is hard to understand why they are not interested in his other resting places. The ancient sources tell us unambiguously that Alexander the Great was laid to rest in 320 by Ptolemy I Soter in a *first* tomb in Memphis, beside the gods of Egypt. On his arrival in Egypt, Alexander had made a point of visiting that city before any of the others, in order to obtain from the priests an initial recognition of his right to the country. Then, the same Ptolemy, after he had proclaimed himself king of Egypt, had a *second* tomb made, this time in his new capital Alexandria. And there was yet a *third* tomb: a century later, one of Soter's descendants, Ptolemy IV Philopator, assembled the mortal remains of his ancestors in one and the same burial place around those of Alexander. Instead of embarking on the search for these three tombs, which are known to have really existed at some point in time and space, people prefer to hunt for them hundreds of miles from Alexandria, from Syria to the oasis of Siwa.

Attempts to find the tomb at Alexandria itself have not been lacking either – far from it! In the last twenty-five years alone there have been more than fifteen of them. The Egyptian authorities have been kind enough to make their records available to me, which show that the 'fools of Alexander' are legion! They include labourers, white-collar workers and a nurse, as well as people described simply as 'citizens'. Their hunches or 'proofs' lead us into various quarters of the city. For instance, on 1 November 1973 the Archaeological Service received a report from a civil servant to the effect that, 'his father-in-law has discovered a cavity in his house (which is owned by Greeks) in the quarter of Camp César; this cavity leads into a corridor faced with marble and he informs the Service that the tomb of Alexander is to be found here' (that is, about one kilometre (two thirds of a mile) east of the quarter of the Ptolemaic palaces, well outside the ancient city walls).

Three years later, in a letter dated 17 January 1976 and addressed to the Egyptian parliament, a labourer recommends that 'it is necessary to save the precious tombs of Ptolemy I, Alexander the Great and Nectanebo II, which are situated underneath the Greek Library; they consist of an ancient, one-storeyed house at 11, Terbana Mosque Street, and belong to a certain Mr Latakie.' The quarter of Gumruk, where this beautiful seventeenth-century mosque still stands, is built on alluvial land which has been forming since the Middle Ages on either side of the Heptastadion, the causeway that connected the island of Pharos with the mainland in antiquity. In other words, the tomb of Alexander would have been in the middle of the Megas Limen,

the Eastern Harbour; we would thus be dealing with an underwater tomb. Another 'discoverer' had located Alexander's tomb quite simply in Sharia Iskander el-Kabir (Alexander-the-Great Street), which would at least prove the durability of this toponym!

One of the best-known searchers, whose memory is still very much alive in Alexandria, was Stelios Coumoutsos. His official dossier of applications for permits and excavation reports contains no less than 322 items from 1956, when he started work, onwards. The enthusiasm of this café waiter was not without effect on some influential people, including the city governor, who gave him permission to conduct several trial excavations. His plans show that he too twice located Alexander's tomb in areas that were under water in antiquity. A photograph showing the amateur archaeologist at the moment of his 'discovery' is captioned: 'The third chamber of the tomb.' A new lead prompted him to excavate in the precinct of the Coptic Cathedral of St Mark opposite Nabi-Danyal Street (we shall return to his reasons for choosing this place – a traditional misunderstanding from the time of the Arab chroniclers of the Renaissance period). On another occasion, the Metropolitan had to call the police to stop Coumoutsos carrying out a trial dig, by night and without permission, in the churchyard of St Saba. Coumoutsos would work for a few years in one of the city's restaurants, amassing a modest sum of money, which he would immediately spend on new excavations. The story of his life, dedicated to the service of Alexander's tomb, deserves to have been told on the menu!

Whether Alexandrians are aware of it or not, the burial place of their city's founder is always there at the back of their minds. Everyone in Alexandria, for instance, can remember how, about ten years ago, a woman disappeared as she was queuing outside a cinema near Nabi-Danyal Street: she was suddenly swallowed up by the earth and her body was never found. The police gave her husband a hard time (even though he had been at her side). One can only suppose that she was carried off by the rainwater which undermines the streets in winter, and drowned in one of the many water channels which still feed the ancient cisterns. Rumour had it, however, that the missing woman had been summoned by Alexander, who wanted a wife.

The interpretation of the sources relating to the location of Alexander's tomb is in fact based on a fundamental confusion: the Arab writers, in particular the most precise of them, Leo the African (early sixteenth century), tell us that many pious Muslims undertook a pilgrimage to the tomb of Alexander (who is one of the prophets recognized by Islam), which lay not far from the Coptic church of St Mark. Nineteenth-century

scholars concluded that the place referred to was the site of the mosque of the prophet (*nabi* in Arabic) Danyal (or Daniel), 300 metres (330 yds) south of the Coptic church. Impressed by the weight of tradition, Mahmud el-Falaki, and even the Italian archaeologist Evaristo Breccia, lost their usual critical acumen and accepted this hypothesis. The identity of this Daniel is uncertain: he could be the Old Testament prophet who died in Babylon in the fifth century BC. The fact that Alexander also breathed his last in Babylon explains why numerous legends have arisen in the course of the centuries, and why the repeated attempts at excavating there – the last application for a permit was submitted by a very respectable professor from Al-Azhar University in 1996 – have encouraged the Alexandrians to believe that the tomb of Alexander and the mosque of Nabi-Danyal were built on the self-same spot.

One has only to climb down into the well which still exists in the middle of the prayer-room to gain certainty. And that is what I did a few years ago with the Imam's kind permission. At the bottom of a shaky ladder I discovered a rotunda with granite columns very like the those at the French Cultural Centre over the road, in the cellars of which a series of columns of the same size, and made of the same kind of stone, have been unearthed. These remains could form part of either a cistern or a colonnade flanking an ancient street, as was common in Alexandria. At any rate, as Rodziewicz has convincingly shown on the basis of his excavations at the neighbouring site of Kom el-Dikka, the altimetric profile of this part of the city definitely rules out the possibility of this being a Ptolemaic level and proves that these monuments belong to the Late Roman period. Finally, the last excavations carried out by the Egyptian Service of Antiquities in this neighbourhood, in 1956, which had as their object the cemetery of Prince Omar Tusun on the south side of the mosque, have brought to light Muslim and then Christian tombs, but, no matter deep the archaeologists dug, they found no Ptolemaic remains.

In fact, a closer examination of el-Falaki's plan of the city's street grid makes it clear that there is no reason to lay so much emphasis on the site of the Nabi-Danyal mosque: all the ancient writers place the tomb in the north-east corner of the crossing of the two principal streets. The identification of this crossroads with the junction of Nabi-Danyal Street and Fuad Street is both arbitrary and illogical, since our sources specifically state that the main north–south street ran from the palaces to the harbour on Lake Mariut, and since el-Falaki's trial trenches did in fact locate two streets at least double the width of the others. They are Fuad Street (or street *L1*, that

The Alabaster Tomb was discovered at the beginning of the twentieth century among the graves of the Catholic cemetery of Terra Santa. Although Adriani extended the excavation when he was director of the Graeco-Roman Museum, he was unable to find anything further in the vicinity. It is to him that we owe the restoration of this monument.

CHAPTER NINE

The catacombs of Kom el-Shuqafa

OPPOSITE: The grave shaft at Kom el-Shuqafa, sunk over 20 metres (65½ ft) into the ground. It is circular, whereas the other tombs at Alexandria usually have square shafts. They were used to lower the corpses and also to provide the hypogea with light.

A circular room traditionally called the 'rotunda'. It plays a central role, giving access to the grave shaft, the banqueting hall and the stairway to the main tomb.

The rock-hewn pillars and parapet surround a further shaft which gives access to a third underground level and to the corridor leading to the main tomb.

BELOW: The façade of the main tomb, with its Egyptian architecture. In the foreground is a scallop shell, a traditional marine motif of the Greek world, unknown in pharaonic Egypt.

OPPOSITE PAGE: Detail of the façade of the main tomb, with its two lotus-shaped columns and its entablature decorated with a winged solar disk. Between the columns can be seen the lintel of the doorway into the burial chapel, with a frieze of rearing cobras and another winged sun disk. In the background, above the central sarcophagus, is a mummification scene.

EVERY TIME ONE VISITS the catacombs of Kom el-Shuqafa, one experiences an unexpected sensation: the temperature remains constant, summer and winter, and the atmosphere is welcoming. And yet, this necropolis is hemmed in by a bustling, noisy, working-class district full of life. After descending a spiral staircase of a hundred steps and arriving about twenty metres (65 ft) below the world of the living on the surface, one finds oneself transported back into the long-gone world of ancient Alexandria.

One is confronted with a chapel loaded, or rather, overloaded with images. Behind its profusion, one senses that each part of the decoration is charged with meaning. The façade of the shallow vestibule is supported on two columns with composite foliate capitals. On the pediment, above a typically pharaonic rounded cornice, there is a relief with two falcons on either side of a winged solar disk. Passing below this, one sees on the left the statue of a standing woman, on the right that of a man. They are almost life-size and presumably portray the owners of the tomb. Their hairstyles date them to the end of the first or the beginning of the second century AD.

To enter the burial chamber, one has to pass through a doorway above which there is a winged disk under a frieze of cobras. On either side of it are circular shields covered with scales and with a Medusa head in the centre (to 'petrify' tomb-robbers), and two snakes (representing the Agathodaimon, the benevolent deity), wearing the double crown of Egypt and coiled around the caduceus of Hermes and the beribboned thyrsus of Dionysus, both Greek symbols.

In the chapel itself, above the sarcophagi in the traditional Greek style with their garlands of leaves and their bunches of grapes, bas-reliefs depict typically Egyptian scenes: the worship of the Apis bull and, in the centre, the mummification of Osiris. The falcon-headed god Horus and the ibis-headed god Thoth flank Anubis, who is embalming the body of Osiris. The latter is lying on a couch in the form of a lion with a raised tail, and three of the four Canopic jars traditionally used to contain the intestines have been placed under it.

Obviously, the inhabitants of a city that had now been under Roman rule for more than a century continued to believe in the old religion of the pharaohs more than 400 years after Egypt had been taken over by Greeks. They had not forgotten the Greek pantheon either, as the references to Hermes and Dionysus and the shield of Athena with Medusa's head in the middle show. Which did they really believe in, these late first-century people: the Egyptian or the Greek gods?

Detail of the right-hand wall of the façade of the main burial chapel. At the top is the head of Medusa, the so-called Gorgoneion, in the centre of Athena's shield. It was believed that Medusa's gaze would turn into stone any intruders who managed to get into the tomb. She is also found on sarcophagi. Below is the Agathodaimon, a protective deity in the form of a long snake. He carries the caduceus of Hermes Psychopompos, the god who accompanies the dead to the afterlife. He also has the thyrsus, the emblem of Dionysus, the god connected with resurrection (Dionysus' other emblem, the vine, also appears as a motif elsewhere in the tomb). The snake is wearing the *pschent*, the pharaonic double crown of Upper and Lower Egypt. The whole composition is a mixture of Greek and Egyptian motifs.

OPPOSITE PAGE: Inside the chapel, on either side of the doorway, an Anubis stands guard. This dog-headed Egyptian deity is linked with death and mummification. Here he is dressed like a Roman legionary, with spear and shield: he too is protecting the dead from intruders. The body of the Anubis on the right as one enters ends in a snake's tail – a kind of physical syncretism between Anubis and Agathodaimon. As we shall also see in the case of the sarcophagi themselves, the tomb's owners evidently wanted a large number of protective devices to guard them against intruders, notably tomb-robbers: Medusa, Agathodaimon and Anubis were to watch together over their last resting place and turn away anyone who threatened to desecrate it.

PREVIOUS PAGES: The interior of the main chapel: two of the three *arcosolia*, niches in which sarcophagi were installed. They are separated from each other by lotus-shaped pilasters; above the niches, a Greek egg-and-tongue frieze is surmounted by the Egyptian motif of a solar disk between two cobras. The decoration of the sarcophagus itself is Greek, with garlands of vines with bunches of grapes, the emblem of Dionysus, the god of resurrection, and also two Medusa heads for protection. On the walls of the niches above the sarcophagi there are scenes in relief of offerings being made to deities and of a mummification.

In the central niche, Anubis is mummifying Osiris. The mummy is lying on a couch in the form of a lion. Horus stands on the viewer's left, Thoth on the right. Under the couch are three Canopic jars. For the dead person, to follow Osiris' example is to hope for resurrection.

OPPOSITE: Above the sarcophagus in the niche on the right, a bas-relief shows a pharaoh offering a pectoral to Apis, the divine bull, who is represented standing on a plinth. On the right, Isis spreads her protective wings over the scene.

PREVIOUS PAGES: The niche on the left contains the same scene as the one facing it. Here is a detail of the offering of the pectoral to the Apis bull. This Memphite deity was worshipped at Alexandria in the sanctuary of Sarapis, a few hundred metres from the necropolis of Kom el-Shuqafa. His cult continued into the Roman period, as is shown by the statue of him dedicated by the Emperor Hadrian.

RIGHT: As the centuries passed, new rooms were hollowed out in the tomb, which remained in use for three centuries, until the fourth century AD. During this time, a large number of dead were laid to rest in the catacombs. The increase in demand led to the installation of a series of new sarcophagi, and above all of *loculi*, niches hollowed lengthwise out of the rock. Some people chose cremation, and at the top left of the photograph can be seen some small niches which held their cinerary urns.

OPPOSITE PAGE: Like the rest of the tomb, the funerary banqueting hall is cut out of the rock, and its four pillars and the benches for the banquet guests are still joined to their limestone bed. This is where the funerary feasts took place – on the day of the funeral, forty days afterwards, on each anniversary and on certain public holidays. The excavators found a large number of pots, bowls and plates, which attest to the custom of these meals eaten in communion with the dead.

The Tomb of Caracalla

In the tomb adjoining the preceding one, a change in the humidity of the atmosphere led a few years ago to the appearance of some painted scenes above the sarcophagi. They can only just be seen on this photograph taken with natural light.

AN ADJACENT TOMB throws some light on this question. Traces of paint have recently been discovered on the stucco panels above its two sarcophagi. I saw these for the first time five years ago, more than a century after the tomb had been excavated. As a result of a rise in the water-table, humidity levels in the tomb had changed, and the surface areas with pigment had reacted differently from unpainted areas.

Above one of the sarcophagi it was possible to distinguish two scenes painted one above the other. The upper zone depicted the mummification of Osiris, as in the tomb described above, but this time painted rather than in bas-relief. It has the same couch in the form of a lion, but Isis and her sister Nephthys have replaced Thoth and Horus on either side of Anubis. The presence of this scene comes as no surprise, considering the decoration of the tomb next door.

The second, lower scene, merits a closer look. It contains three figures gesturing animatedly, with swirling, pleated garments. One of them is a

helmeted woman, brandishing a spear and a shield; she must be Athena, and this is therefore a Greek painting. Although the figures were very faint, I was gradually able to make out two more women: could the subject be the Judgment of Paris? (According to this well-known Greek myth, Athena, Hera and Aphrodite let the young Trojan herdsman decide which of them was the most beautiful. His choice of Aphrodite aroused the envy of the other two goddesses and led to the Trojan war.) But what could this story, which has no connection with the rites of the dead, be doing in this tomb? The use of artificial lighting was to solve the problem. It took a team several weeks to interpret the scene with the help of ultra-violet spotlights worked by André Pelle.

The archaeologists Anne-Marie Guimier-Sorbets and Mervat Seif el-Din shut themselves in, together with the draughtswoman Mary-Jane Schumacher, for hours at a time to try to make out the details. The female figures appeared clearly (the longer one looks, the clearer and more certain the

Using ultra-violet light, and with the help of photography and drawings, the archaeologists were able to bring out the evanescent scenes, establishing that the scene below the upper, Egyptian, register was a Greek one. In the upper field a mummification like that in the preceding tomb is taking place, with Anubis in the middle, behind the lion-shaped couch on which the mummy lies. Below this, a group of Greek goddesses can be made out: Artemis on the left, brandishing her bow, Athena with spear and shield, and Aphrodite with Eros perched on her shoulder. Unfortunately, the passage that has been dug through the wall into the neighbouring tomb has deprived us of the right-hand part of the scene.

A few metres away, opposite the sarcophagus niche shown in the preceding photographs, ultra-violet light revealed another wall-painting – even fainter than the first – above another sarcophagus. It has the same arrangement in two registers, with the mummification of Osiris in the upper one and, in the lower one, the complete Greek scene. On the right, a four-horse chariot in rapid motion is being guided by Hades, who is carrying off a struggling woman. She must be Persephone, the daughter of Demeter. He wants to take her down to the Underworld with him, to her mother's despair. But Zeus will arrange a compromise that will allow the young woman to return to the surface of the earth for six months of the year, before returning again to her husband's underground realm. This double register corresponds to the double belief in an afterlife expressed by the two religions of the Alexandrians at the beginning of the second century AD.

These oil sketches are the work of M.-J. Schumacher, who spent weeks in Tomb 2 at Kom el-Shuqafa, with the archaeologists A.-M. Guimier-Sorbets and M. Seif el-Din and the photographer A. Pelle, in order to interpret these scenes, which are almost invisible to the naked eye.

details become, confirming what could previously be only partially seen with the naked eye): Athena holds her weapons in the middle, flanked on her left by Aphrodite with Eros on her shoulder, and on her right, not by Hera, but by Artemis drawing her bow. Moreover, Paris is not to be seen. Instead, to the right of the goddesses (i.e. on their left), a head can be seen, bent to the left and wearing a *kalathos*, a tall headdress symbolizing prosperity and worn by certain goddesses, such as Demeter and her daughter Persephone. Unfortunately, the scene breaks off there because the first excavators of the tomb made a hole here between the sarcophagi to gain access to the tomb next door. It looked as though the significance of the scene was to elude us for ever.

Luckily, we decided to shine the UV lamps into the adjoining niches. Under this lighting, the very same scenes, one above the other, appeared totally unexpectedly on the wall above another sarcophagus. In the upper register we recognized the mummification of Osiris; in the lower, the Greek scene is intact – and it provides the key to what is going on. The three goddesses stand on the viewer's left; the bent head with the *kalathos* belongs to a woman being carried off in a four-horse chariot by a bearded figure: it is Hades abducting Persephone and taking her to his kingdom in the Underworld. On the side walls, two scenes complete the story of the abduction: one shows Persephone before the event, in the company of her friends; the other her reappearance from the mouth of the cave leading to

the Underworld under the eyes of her mother and of Hecate. This interpretation is beyond doubt: Demeter's daughter leaves the surface of the earth against her will, but soon, faced with her mother's despair, Hades is prepared to compromise. Every year, Persephone is to spend six months in the Underworld with her new husband, and to return in spring to the upper world to be reunited with her mother. Just like the mummifying of Osiris, Persephone's disappearance to the Underworld is the prelude to a rebirth in the land of the living.

The interesting thing about the tombs of Kom el-Shuqafa is obviously the juxtaposition of two different types of scene, one above the other. The syncretism of Greek religion has often been remarked upon: the population accepted without difficulty the gods of their neighbours. In Egypt itself, deities unfamiliar to the new immigrants from the Mediterranean were found an equivalent in the Greek pantheon: Hathor became Aphrodite, and Thoth the local version of Hermes. In these tombs, however, there is no mixing – the style of the paintings itself rules out any confusion – but, rather, a superimposition or an addition of the two divine worlds. The dead of Alexandria show us that it was possible to place oneself under the protection of two systems of belief that were alien to each other. Everything therefore points to the conclusion that, over and beyond all the syncretism and equivalence, it was possible in the ancient capital of the Ptolemies to adhere to two religions as different as the Greek and the pharaonic, in the hope not only of a harmonious life in the hereafter, but even of a rebirth, of a resurrection. In this period, moreover, at the beginning of the second century AD, a new religion, that of Christ, was spreading in the city, one which stated clearly that it was the destiny of every human being one day to rise again.

This ring was found during the Second World War by Alan Rowe, who conducted some very fruitful digs at the Sarapeion and also at Kom el-Shuqafa. He was fortunate enough to discover an unpillaged tomb which had escaped the attentions both of the tomb-robbers and of his predecessors. Inside the sarcophagus, he found the mummy of a woman with golden jewellery, including this ring. The intaglio shows the union of Leda and the swan, the 'sacred marriage' between the wife of Tyndareus, king of Sparta, and Zeus, king of the gods, from which the Dioscuri were to spring.

CHAPTER TEN

The Necropolis (Gabbari)

OPPOSITE: Gabbari, Tomb 1 by night, with (top) the threat of the major road under construction in the background.

This plaster head of Medusa, one of the finds from the excavation of the necropolis, was supposed to discourage people from desecrating the tombs. She has kept some colour: blue round the eyes and red on the lips (Ptolemaic period).

OPPOSITE PAGE: The bulldozer had been digging away at the rock, preparing for the construction of the road, until the moment when this first tomb was discovered. Such an important discovery led to a temporary halt in the construction work.

BELOW: View of the excavation site below the flyover, the surface of which stops abruptly.

O N THURSDAY 26 JUNE 1997, the Director General of the Museums and Archaeological Sites of Alexandria, Ahmed Abdel Fattah, asked me to accompany him, together with a photographer from the CEA, on an inspection tour of several sites which had just been discovered by chance in the course of some public works. We set out for the Antoniadis Gardens in the south-east of the city, where a large, and complete, column of Aswan granite lies in the middle of a lawn. We continued through the Mustafa Kamal district, where some tombs with both inhumations and intact cinerary urns of the Greek period had just been discovered.

We finally reached the district of Gabbari in the west, where the construction of a flyover (built to connect the desert road from Cairo to Alexandria with the Western Harbour) had been halted a few hundred metres from its northern end. The rest of the construction, about a kilometre in length, was almost finished, but the contractors had hit upon an obstacle: a large Hellenistic tomb had been uncovered by the mechanical diggers during the excavation of a trench for one of the piles of the flyover.

It had proved almost impossible to do anything about it for lack of agreement on the financing between the contractors and the Archaeological Service.

At the end of the financial year, which in Egypt falls in June, subsidies for emergency digs are hard to come by. The Director of Antiquities asked me if the CEA would be able to step in. Fortunately, our own financial year ends in December, and I still had some funds left. On the basis of a quick calculation that the weekly cost of an operation of this nature would be 25,000 francs (approx. £2,500), and that the excavation would take two weeks, I agreed.

On Saturday 28 June, just two days after our first visit, four archaeologists, a topographer, two draughtswomen, a photographer and three restorers, all from the CEA, started on the excavation of the group of tombs visible from the surface. They were assisted by about forty workers with several years' training in stratigraphy and experience of working on emergency digs in the city centre. They all knew that speed was essential, because the period of grace granted to archaeologists is short. Once handed back to the contractor, the tomb would be destroyed; there could be no question of returning later to check some detail or other. But our team was used to the discipline this imposed: on the very first day, a plan of this part of the necropolis was made and the excavation got under way.

This request for a rescue operation is typical of the kind of surprise that the soil of Alexandria regularly produces. For the developer it is an unpleasant surprise, since he is obliged to stop work because of the importance of the remains he has just uncovered. It is also a surprise for the archaeologists, who have to cope with unexpected discoveries for which no allowance has been made in their budgets, and this can involve delays detrimental to their work.

The plans drawn up in the nineteenth century, when Alexandria was not nearly as big as it is now, show that the ancient city and its necropoleis extend under practically the whole of the modern built-up area. As we have seen, Mahmud el-Falaki's plan clearly shows the street grid and the course of the Graeco-Roman city walls. The ancient urban area was densely built up, while the main east–west artery is more than five kilometres (3 miles) long within the city walls. Once through the gates in the walls, the necropoleis begin: in the west, those of Gabbari, Wardian, Mex; in the east, Shatby, Hadra, Eleusis and, beyond them, Sidi Gaber, Mustafa Kamal, Rushdy. Even further to the east, remains of various isolated monuments have been found: rural sanctuaries, like the temples of Ras el-Soda and Montaza, or

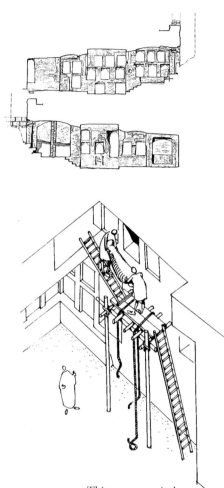

OPPOSITE PAGE: Tomb 1 with its 230 *loculi*.

UPPER DIAGRAM: This axonometrical drawing is by the architect Olivier Callot. It shows the extent of the chambers and the different levels of their *loculi*.

LOWER DIAGRAM: By studying the dowel holes in the walls of Tomb 8, Callot was able to reconstruct the wooden scaffolding which was used to reach the upper rows of *loculi*.

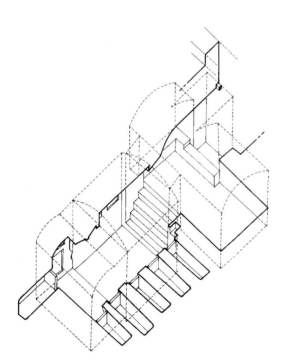

The architect Olivier Callot has studied the different phases in the arrangement of the tombs and has been able to produce this section drawing of the north and south sides of the collective tomb no. 2, in its third phase of enlargement.

these caves and these holes, and to what purpose I believe them to have been made. To which I shall reply that it is very difficult to say exactly, seeing that Macrizi, who has otherwise given a very exact description of everything of interest in Egypt, does not mention them. Nonetheless, one can see that they cannot have served as anything other than burial chambers. That is clear from the form of the holes, which are exactly the right length, height and width for a coffin to be placed in them. And then, as all the other caves in Egypt served only this purpose, it is probable that these caves were made to the same end. And so I leave the reader to form his own judgement of this.'

One and a half centuries later Constantine of Kiev visited some tombs eroded by the sea which appear on engravings of the period under the name of 'the baths of Cleopatra': 'Huge cliffs jut out from the shore; sinister gorges form a wild-looking collection of natural caverns; and what is more, because of the convenience of this natural situation and the kind of soft stone [of which these cliffs are formed], veritable rooms have been dug out of the cliff. They were used [by the locals] as baths and as shelters for boats in bad weather.'

There follows a description of a tomb so huge that the writer takes it to be a subterranean temple: through a long corridor 'one enters a round chamber with smooth, polished walls and ceiling and a floor covered in sand and all kinds of rubbish, and inhabited by bats and every kind of vermin. But this is not yet the temple; another underground corridor leads into a circular room with a ceiling hewn in the shape of a vault and four doors facing each other; each of them is decorated with a cornice and above the pediment of each is a crescent [moon]. One of these four doors is open, whereas the other three form recesses in the walls with a lower floor level than the temple and each contains a receptacle cut in the rock, which is now empty, [but], it seems, was once the tomb of a famous man or a tsar [emperor].'

Constantine adds that the other corridors which could be glimpsed had partly caved in and were inaccessible; he also mentions 'some pits', which had been dug on the top of the cliff, 'about sixty feet deep and twenty feet wide, but now filled with rubbish.'

Napoleon's scholars also visited this large tomb and drew a plan of it. One can still read the detailed descriptions of the necropolis which Gratien Le Père and D. G. Dolomieu have left us.

Another visitor to the necropolis, a member of the French Academy named Michaud, who went there in 1831, notes: 'It is customary with

PREVIOUS PAGES AND OPPOSITE:
These photographs give an idea
of the state of the tombs at the
time of their discovery. Rain and
wind have frequently filled them
with sand, which has protected
them. The rows of *loculi* can be
seen: the niches measure about
70 centimetres (27 in) across
and are 2 metres (6½ ft) long.
Up to seven rows can be
counted, one above the other;
the larger tombs may contain
more than 200 *loculi*.

smallest possible space? This becomes clear from the story which repeats itself in every tomb. Originally, a well-off man has a tomb made for himself, with an atrium open to the sky, a flight of steps leading down into it and a sarcophagus in a chamber with painted decoration. But then one day, he is turned out: his sarcophagus is removed so that the first *loculi* can be hollowed out of the walls; then new chambers are cut out of the rock on the other sides of the atrium: one occupant makes way for a hundred, or even many more. The *loculi* were closed with a limestone slab sealed with plaster. Frequently, however, a *loculus* was reopened, the first occupant pushed to the back and another corpse placed beside him. This procedure must have been repeated many times; we have found up to ten skeletons in a single *loculus*.

Yet this concern to house so many corpses in a small space can be explained, not by lack of room (Strabo was amazed by the acreage of the cemetery area, which he refers to as the Necropolis, or 'city of the dead'), but by the exceptional size of the city itself. Admittedly, estimates of its population differ; the lower ones put it at 400,000, the higher at a million. Flavius Josephus writes that the city's Jewish minority alone numbered more than a million, but that would give a truly astronomical total figure!

Like all statistics that people attempt to draw up for antiquity, demographic estimates depend on juggling with a few numbers provided in an irregular and almost accidental fashion by writers using exaggerated language to describe their astonishment at the unusually large size of a settlement. This lack of data can only provoke a pitying smile from the demographers of the modern world; the historian of the ancient world has to battle with hypotheses which often cannot be reconciled with each other. One example will suffice: some people estimate the population of the island of Delos in the early first century at 25,000 inhabitants, while others calmly point out that, if the relative proportion of free citizens to slaves is taken into account, the number of individuals ought to exceed 100,000, or four times as many. It is obviously a great pity that the ancient registers which served various purposes in the running of the state and of the city have not survived: people had their children registered with the magistrates, who declared them citizens if they were born of Greek parents who were themselves born citizens, while other registers facilitated the collection of taxes. Most of these lists, however, were kept on papyrus, and no papyri have been found in the excavations at Alexandria because they do not survive in its climate.

The recent excavations of dwellings in the heart of the city suggest we

Sometimes the name of the dead person is written above the *loculus*, with a brief farewell message. A certain Dionysia was buried here. All the inscriptions are in Greek, and the names are also Greek.

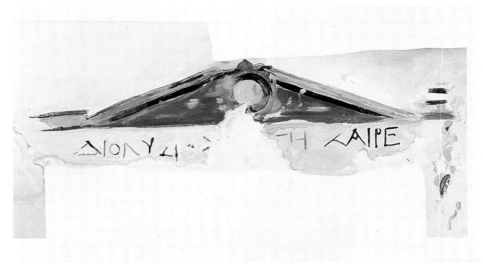

The *loculi* were sealed with painted slabs. They usually represent a double door, symbolically closed. They are brightly painted and must be copies of the doors of real Alexandrian houses (the reconstruction drawing below was made during the excavation).

should keep to a low estimate of the population size. The residential character of the big houses uncovered on the site of the Diana Theatre and the former British Consulate confirm this. These buildings have nothing in common with the multi-storeyed investment properties with which we are familiar from Rome or Ostia. Admittedly, the houses at Alexandria are in a fashionable district, less than a kilometre from the royal palaces, but the built-up area remains well-spaced everywhere, which again suggests we should keep to the lower figure. Even so, 400,000 inhabitants made Alexandria the most populous city of the Hellenistic world, surpassed only by imperial Rome.

When Strabo arrived at Alexandria in 25 BC, three centuries had passed since its foundation. The city had developed very rapidly. If one counts twenty-five years as a generation, as historical demographers do, one realizes that during these three centuries several million dead people must have been buried. At the same time, one understands why Strabo was amazed at the vastness of this cemetery, and why the undertakers were forced to look for every available bit of space to provide the dead Alexandrians with a last resting place. Thanks to the various physical remains and the inscriptions they left, we know that these undertakers conceived and put into practice an architectural solution exactly suited to the city's needs. What is more, they made a double profit from this method, for the grooves in the *loculi* that had been in the process of being hollowed out show that the blocks extracted had been cut free with care so that they could be offered for sale as building material for the city of the living.

Our excavation of the *loculi* has turned out to be fruitful: the anthropologists now have hundreds of skeletons at their disposal which will enable them to study a cross-section of the population. From these bones, they will be able to calculate a person's height; determine their age at death, their sex and, in the case of women, the number of times they gave birth; check the state of their teeth; identify certain illnesses, and find out whether they had undergone any surgery. In this way a whole new side of the lives of the Greeks of Alexandria is being revealed.

The people buried in this part of the necropolis were actually Greeks. This is shown by their names (like those mentioned above, Dionysia and Marion) and by certain funerary customs. In one of the rooms of Tomb 1, a *loculus* contained a skeleton with a little bronze coin inside the skull. This is the obolus which the Greeks piously placed in the dead person's mouth so that he could pay his fare to the ferryman Charon and be sure of getting across the Styx, the river which separated the Underworld from the land of the living.

OPPOSITE PAGE: One of the slabs used to close the *loculi* is painted with a scene in which a standing man clasps the hand of a woman sitting facing him. It is a *dexiosis* (a clasping of the right hand in farewell), a scene which is to be found on the grave stelae of classical Athens. Here, it is superimposed on the double doors which appear to be a standard motif on these slabs.

This amphora from Gaza served as a simple coffin for a child who lived in the fourth century AD.

OPPOSITE PAGE: In each *loculus* at least one skeleton has been found. Most of them were reopened and the first occupant pushed aside to make way for another corpse. In the *loculus* seen here, on the right of the latest arrival, three skulls of previous occupants can be seen. We have counted up to ten skeletons in one *loculus*.

Besides the *loculi* designed for inhumations, shallower niches were cut in the rock to hold cinerary urns, several examples of which have been found. These are called Hadra hydrias (or Hadra vases) by archaeologists, and are a kind of water jar with one vertical and two horizontal handles. They get their name from a cemetery to the east of Alexandria, in the area of the ancient lake of Hadra, where a large number of them have been found. They are about 40 centimetres (16 in) high, and are decorated with geometric

In the photograph on the previous page, one can see a little round dot in the skull of the skeleton. It is easier to see in this photograph of a head from another tomb that this is a small bronze coin. It is the obolus which, in accordance with Greek custom, was placed in the dead person's mouth, so that he could pay Charon, the ferryman who would bring him over the River Styx which separated the Underworld from the world of the living.

OPPOSITE PAGE: Several *loculi* contained offerings to the dead: terracotta lamps, which were often decorated with mythological motifs; little spindle-shaped vases filled with perfumed oil; incense altars; and statuettes of women and children, and of Alexandrian deities, like the little Harpocrates on the left. These objects are in an excellent state of preservation – they were used only once. Instead of the fragments that archaeologists normally find in their excavations, they now have a selection of unbroken vases to choose from.

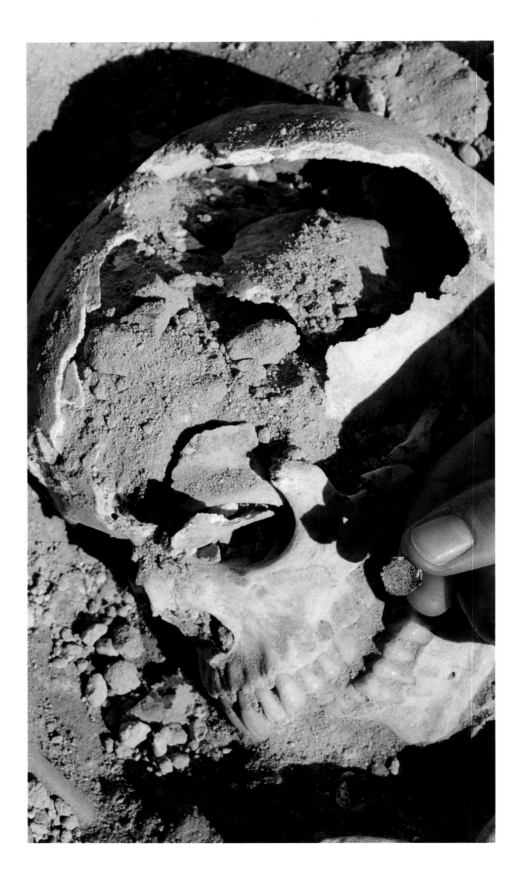

and floral motifs. Most of them come from Crete, as clay analyses have shown, and date from the second half of the third century BC. We already have about five hundred of them, dispersed in museums in Egypt and the West. These vases sometimes have inscriptions referring to Greeks from elsewhere who had died during an official visit to the Alexandrian authorities. They had been cremated by the magistrates, doubtless at the city's expense, and their ashes collected in these hydrias.

Many of these vases, however, have no inscription. It is likely that some Alexandrians chose this form of burial either because of their beliefs or out of economic necessity. In fact, cremation and inhumation existed side by side in the Greek world, whereas inhumation with mummification was the only standard practice among the Egyptians (as later among the Christians), for whom cremation was taboo because it prevented the dead person from being reborn.

Returning to the tomb, several steps lead down to a lower

PREVIOUS PAGES: View of the main chamber of the collective Tomb 3, the lower part of which is below the water-table as a result of the general subsidence of the ground level at Alexandria. This photograph shows how considerable this has been. The divers from the Pharos site were able to use their equipment to explore the lower levels of the tomb. The steps in the background lead to the atrium (or air well), the only area open to the sky.

Some Greeks chose to have themselves cremated, and the excavations have produced evidence for this. Here is a selection of Hadra hydrias, jars which contained the charred remains of bodies. They were placed in little niches cut in the rock, near the *loculi* intended for inhumations. Anthropologists specializing in cremation burial have been able to examine the contents of these jars and determine the sex, age and illnesses of their occupants. One has been identified as a woman, whereas it had previously been thought that the jars contained only male burials. Sometimes, the name of the dead person, that of the magistrate who authorized the cremation, and the date of death are painted or engraved on the shoulder of the jar. The jars were usually decorated with vegetal or geometric motifs, sometimes with figures (mid-third century BC).

BC and establishes a link between the offerings made to the dead man and his activities in life. In a similar manner, the little lamps, of which around five hundred have been found so far, depict figures from Greek mythology, especially Aphrodite and Eros, in this case linking Eros with Thanatos (Death).

The burial objects are abundant; apparently the tomb robbers were interested only in valuable items. We may not have found many jewels, but we have found hundreds of perfectly preserved vases of fired clay. They were brought here as offerings to the dead, used once and then left, so they are in

This Hadra vase shows a hunting scene: on the left is a beribboned caduceus, the symbol of Hermes Psychopompos, the conductor of souls to the Underworld, and to the right of it, a naked man, seen in three-quarter view from the back, holding a long lance. In front of him a hunting dog is attacking a cervid with long horns, apparently an ibex, while another dog attacks it from

one piece and undamaged, in contrast to the fragments we usually find during our rescue digs in the homes of the living, where we uncover only discarded items which are broken into small pieces and often carry the signs of having been well used before being thrown out.

The objects offered to the dead are mainly oil lamps, little incense altars and also *unguentaria* (small, tapering vases which contained perfumed oils). We have also found sets of tableware (plates and bowls), which remind us of the stores of food left in front of the tombs – mainly oil, wheat and wine. These offerings were often made during the funerary meals which families used to organize in honour of their dead. On the day of the funeral, on the fortieth day after that, and on various fixed holidays in the city's calendar,

behind. The attitude of the dogs, their mouths wide open for the attack and their tails between their hind legs, expresses tension and a fear of danger. This lively scene is the work of one of the Cretan potters who exported their wares to the Ptolemies' capital (mid-third century BC).

Two oil lamps from among the hundreds found in the Gabbari tombs. Top: Eros clinging on to the mane of a lion. Bottom: Aphrodite doing her hair, following a classical model. The motifs that decorate these lamps come from Greek mythology. Their theme is often love linked with death – Eros and Thanatos (first century BC).

people gathered together in a funerary dining-room like one we uncovered just below the surface.

A long bench, hewn out of the rock, runs round three walls of the room. On it would be placed the mattresses on which the guests would recline. In the same room, a series of cups and plates and also some wine amphorae have been found. They contained not local wine, but one of the best vintages of the Mediterranean, which was of course served to show honour to the dead, but also suggests that these feasts were boozy affairs – rather like funeral feasts in rural France or Irish wakes, from which the participants often come away inebriated (understandable, considering that the community of survivors is trying to expunge the memory of its close encounter with death and to regain the feeling that life is worth living).

The way the collective tombs of the necropolis are constructed shows that we are dealing with the dead of the middle classes – no sumptuous decoration, no really stunning paintings. But discoveries are unpredictable, and with the extension of the excavations northwards we may come across other kinds of tombs. The projected route of the new road means that we

Just below the surface, and miraculously spared by the bulldozers, this funerary banqueting room belongs to a collective tomb. It is easily recognizable as such by the benches cut out of the rock on three of its sides. Mattresses were placed on them for the diners who were sharing – symbolically – a meal with their departed dear ones. These meals took place on the day of the funeral, forty days after the death and on its anniversaries and on certain fixed feast days when the dead were honoured.

ABOVE AND ABOVE LEFT: A collection of deep dishes found in the funerary banqueting room. Wine amphorae from the Greek islands of Rhodes and Cos have also been found. They show that choice wines flowed freely at these feasts.

shall be excavating right up to the Western Harbour, more than 200 metres (220 yds) from the spot where we are now. So far we have uncovered only a fifth of the area to be investigated, and we can still hope for all sorts of discoveries. We have been told, for instance, about a tomb near the quay, not far from where Henri Riad excavated the famous tomb with the *saqieh* mentioned above.

These tombs were made around the middle of the third century BC, to judge from their grave goods, although at the moment it is difficult to say more precisely when the necropolis was begun. At any rate, we are dealing with the first generations of Alexandrians: if not the very first, then the second. As for the systematic exploitation of the place, it must have started fairly early, judging by the scarcity of objects from the Roman period. The tombs seem to have been treated with respect for a long time, and it is not until the fourth century that evidence for their reoccupation is found.

In two of the tombs, there are painted crosses on the walls and the ceiling, and even some stuccoed stelae covered in Christian symbols. Inscriptions give us the names of the dead, including that of a certain Isidora (a

Several tombs were reoccupied during the Christian period. The persecutions ordered by the Emperor Diocletian were particularly violent at Alexandria, and the Christians sought refuge in the hypogea, where they installed their churches and also buried their dead, as shown by this cross on the frame of a *loculus*.

OPPOSITE PAGE, TOP: The offerings to the dead did not change over the centuries. Like their ancestors seven hundred years earlier, the Christians of the third century BC continued to offer lamps to their dead. They are no longer decorated with mythological scenes, however, but with simple crosses.

OPPOSITE PAGE, BOTTOM: Pilgrims' water bottles (St Menas flasks) also feature among the funerary objects of the Christian period. They bear an image of the saint, dressed as a Roman soldier, between two camels. These flasks of baked clay contained the miracle-working water that people took away with them as a souvenir of their pilgrimage to his monastery, which lay about fifty kilometres (30 miles) south-west of Alexandria. Numerous examples have been found all round the Mediterranean and attest to the popularity of this holy place between the fourth and ninth centuries AD.

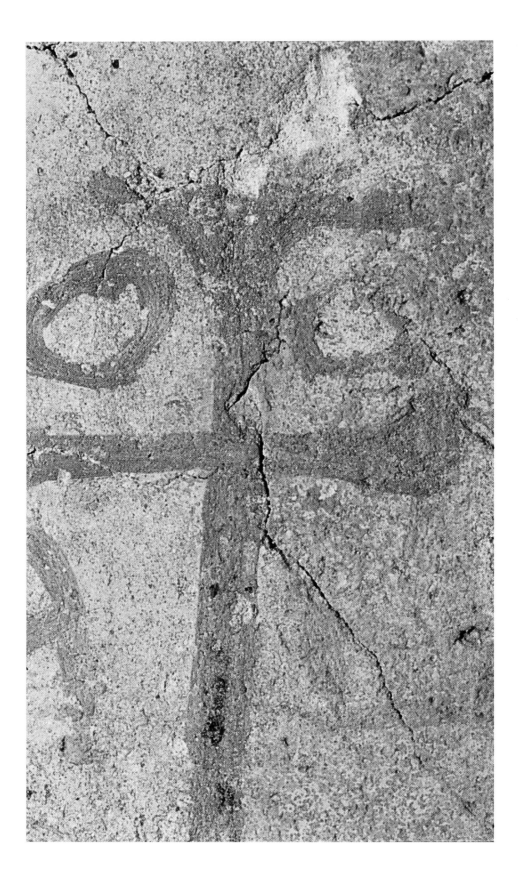

good Graeco-Egyptian name). It is well known that in AD 293 the Christians, of whom there were many at Alexandria, where the Church was firmly established, became the target of a particularly savage persecution unleashed by the Emperor Diocletian. The severity of the massacre shocked the population so much that it has left its imprint on the Coptic calendar, which counts the years starting from 'the Era of Martyrs', this infamous year, 293. That is why in AD 1998 we find ourselves in the year 1715 of the Christian calendar of Egypt.

The *History of the Fathers of the Church of Alexandria* tells how the Christians were forced to take refuge in the tombs of the necropolis, where they installed churches; and archaeology in its turn teaches us that they buried their dead there. The offerings, however, changed hardly at all with the advent of the Christians: they consist of terra-cotta lamps (now adorned with crosses); wine amphorae, mostly from Gaza; and little flasks containing water from the sanctuary of St Menas, about fifty kilometres (30 miles) south-east of Alexandria (the saint is represented on them with his hands raised in prayer between two camels kneeling at his feet; see p. 239).

(the saint is represented on them with his hands raised in prayer between two camels kneeling at his feet; see p. 239).

Let us return to our tour through the holes of the tomb-robbers. This time, we emerge in a large chamber in which we can stand upright. Part of the ceiling has collapsed and the rest is threatening to do so. Thanks to a new staircase, we can climb on to a sort of mezzanine. In a corner, one can see a ray of light shining through another tomb-robbers' hole: there must be a way to the open air up there.

We have already visited three tombs. In the middle of the north wall of the honey-combed chamber, a narrow corridor leads to a fourth tomb, in which, in a long vaulted chamber, the remains of a painted ceiling of the Ptolemaic period can be seen. On the floor there is an infant burial: the skeleton is curled up in a terracotta amphora. In a corner of the room, we climb a narrow tomb-robbers' passage. We hope to find new tombs – unrobbed ones this time.

Six months of work have gone by since the start of the excavation and we are a fifth of the way through it. It is a very moving sensation to pass from one tomb to the next in the path of the ancient tomb-robbers through this interminable 'Swiss cheese'. So far, we have counted seventeen tombs, and we are trying not to let ourselves get carried away. How far will these subterranean passages lead us through this city of the dead which lies under present-day Alexandria? Where are its limits? Are there yet more levels under our feet, which we may be fortunate enough to glimpse before the excavation has to be abandoned? It is enough to make one feel dizzy!

OPPOSITE PAGE: This remarkable tomb is one of the excavation's most recent discoveries. The atrium has a Doric entablature with triglyphs and metopes, while the principal chamber has Ionic columns.

ABOVE: This ceiling, in another tomb, is decorated with a central field of geometric motifs surrounded by a frieze of winged cupids and dolphins.

CHAPTER ELEVEN

The environs of Alexandria

OPPOSITE: The Delta begins on the eastern shore of Lake Mariut. This aerial view of it, taken from a helicopter, shows a modern canal running alongside the lake, following the example of the ancient canals.

The site of Philoxenite, on the southern shore of Lake Mariut.

One of the many wine-presses found on the south bank of Lake Mariut. They belonged to the wine-growing villas that began to develop in the Ptolemaic period and expanded rapidly in Roman times. They produced a well-known wine, which was praised by such famous poets as Virgil and Horace.

the canal of Alexandria, south-west of the Sarapeion – its traces are marked on the map of the city made by Napoleon's scholars.

On the shores adjoining the city, docks, quays and warehouses were built. This explains why Strabo could regard the harbour on the lake at Alexandria as even more important than the maritime harbours: 'The advantages of the city's site are various; for, first, the place is washed by two seas, on the north by the Egyptian Sea as it is called, and on the south by Lake Mareia, also called Mareotis. This is filled by many canals from the Nile, both from above and on the sides, and through these canals the imports are much larger than those from the sea, so that the harbour on the lake was in fact richer than that on the sea.'[45]

The level of the water in the lake has varied considerably over the years. In the Roman period, as Strabo notes,[46] Lake Mariut received water from the Nile flood. Since the end of antiquity, however, the level has not stopped falling, with the result that the eastern part of the lake has dried up and given

way to cultivated land. It was here that in 1801 the English made a dyke separating the lake from Lake Edku on its east, with the aim of getting the French troops under General Menou bogged down (as Saint-Genis tells us, they submerged about twenty villages). Today, the water level is more than a metre (3 ft) lower than in the Graeco-Roman period, as is shown by the fact that the ancient harbour installations have been left partly high and dry.

THIS SEMI-ARID AREA was ideal for looking for ancient structures and remains, and that is what I set out to do together with Maurice Picon in 1977. On a tour round the edge of the lake, we were able to establish the existence of around thirty sites. The most obvious on the surface were the rubbish dumps of workshops that made wine amphorae. This was an interesting discovery, because the existence of this kind of industry had not been suspected, and because Egypt had been believed to be unsuitable for the production of this type of vessel, the reason given being its lack of clay! These piles of sherds proved the contrary; some heaps reached impressive proportions: 10 metres high by 30 metres long (33 × 100 ft). They showed that a great number of amphorae had been broken there. That they had actually been produced on these sites, not just used and discarded, is proved by the presence of numerous wasters, and even by remains of kilns. A preliminary typological classification carried out on the spot suggests that production goes back to the Ptolemaic period and that it continued for nearly a thousand years until after the Arab conquest in 640. These amphorae explain the presence of the hundreds of complete examples that have been in the Graeco-Roman Museum for decades: in addition to the large quantities of wine imported from the Greek islands, the Alexandrians were also fond of drinking the produce of their own hinterland.

These initial discoveries in the area confirm the writings of ancient authors. Strabo praised the wines grown on the lake: 'the vintages in this region are so good that the Mareotic wine is racked off with a view to ageing it.'[47] In other words, it was regarded as a wine for keeping, and was drunk only after several years, like the best Greek vintages.

Strabo is not alone in his appreciation of the wine of Lake Mariut. Its praises are sung by some eminent ancient authors. Among them are Alexandrians, such as Bishop Clement or Athenaeus (both second to third century); but they are not just

Ceramics and viticulture

This silver goblet chased with gold belongs to the collection of the Graeco-Roman Museum in Alexandria. It shows cupids harvesting grapes, treading them in a press and collecting the juice in a container, surrounded by a pattern of vines. This Dionysiac scene testifies to the fertility of the Alexandrian countryside, which produced a popular wine (first century AD).

being chauvinistic, since Horace and Virgil, Pliny the Elder and Catullus all express a similar opinion. This means that the wine of Lake Mariut was already being exported from the end of the first century BC onwards, even as far as Rome, where it graced the dining-tables of the best circles.

One piece of archaeological evidence for the popularity of Mareotic wine in the West comes from a wreck discovered in the Golfe de Fos near Marseilles: dozens of amphorae like those from the rubbish dumps of the lakeside workshops now adorn the showcases in the museums of Provence. They give us some idea of the volume of the wine exported from the Mareotis, even to distant places such as the Rhone valley.

To maintain such exports, the region around the lake must have presented a very different appearance from that of today: it was covered with vineyards and populated with the large number of people needed to tend them.

Recent excavations

RECENT EXCAVATIONS HAVE CONFIRMED these assumptions. From 1985 onwards, the development of Alexandria's industrial zone towards the west, then the proliferation of weekend cottages, and finally the digging of a new canal in the region of Abu Mina (50 km to the south-west) have changed the countryside drastically and led to a need for archaeological salvage operations, which are carried out by the Egyptian Archaeological Service – at any rate, when the owners of the land declare their chance finds.

Several sites where amphorae were made have been uncovered, complete with kilns and areas for drying and storage. Some have impressive structures. For instance, it has been possible to excavate and make accessible to the public the largest Roman kiln known to date. It is about 12 metres (40 ft) in diameter and several hundred amphorae could be fired in it in one go. This gives some idea of the annual production of such workshops.

Besides the workshops producing amphorae, several wine-presses were unearthed. They are all made to the same design and have an area for treading the grapes from which the must flows directly into a deep vat through an opening in the form of a lion's head made of limestone or marble (a recurring feature of all these presses). The Graeco-Roman Museum has a collection of similar 'gargoyles'; they are doubtless from wine-presses now lost which once stood dotted around the countryside near Alexandria. The vats had a capacity of several cubic metres and could hold 20–50 hl (70–176 cubic ft) of must. These large quantities are unusual in the Greek world. The Greeks of Alexandria, and after them the Romans, must have abandoned the traditional Greek way of doing things and adopted the Egyptian methods of winemaking, which were doubtless better suited to the country's climate.

The must fermented in the vat, where it had to stay for a few days; then it was poured directly into the amphorae. To prevent a second fermentation starting up as a result of the heat and bursting the vessels, a small hole was made in the neck of the amphora to allow gases to escape. There was also a

small press near the area where the grapes were trodden, which shows what care was taken that none of the harvest should be wasted, in spite of the huge quantities of grapes being processed. Nowhere else in the Greek world have such large fermentation vats been found.

As well as the wine-presses, wine-growing villas have been found in several places. Some, dating from the Imperial period, are of an impressive size and luxuriousness, and their owners were obviously prosperous. These spacious homes are equipped with private baths, their walls faced with slabs of imported marble.

For some years now, as the rescue work progresses, the picture of the ancient landscape of the Mareotis has been pieced together. There is little left of it in these areas, however, which even recently were still semi-desert. One has to remember that in the Graeco-Roman period conditions were

This kiln for firing amphorae is one of the largest known from antiquity. It measures 12 metres (39 ft) across at the base and could fire several hundred amphorae at a time: these would then be used to transport the produce of the Mareotic vineyards across the lake to Alexandria, or to destinations further afield. A wreck carrying amphorae from here has been found in the Golfe de Fos at the mouth of the Rhône (second century AD).

different: the land was divided up between big wine-growing properties, and the wine production was concentrated near the shores of the lake, where the full amphorae were loaded on to boats to supply the nearby metropolis and the rest of the Mediterranean.

AT INTERVALS ALONG THE SHORES of Lake Mariut lie several small towns: Taposiris and Plinthine on the north, and Philoxenite on the south shore. As regards remains and chronology, each is interesting in its own way.

The towns of the Mareotis

PREVIOUS PAGES: Inside the precinct of the sanctuary of Osiris at Taposiris Magna. This temple was built by Ptolemy II in the mid-third century BC and converted into a Roman camp during the fourth century AD. The ruins of a church can be seen in the middle of the camp, and, in the background, the Mediterranean.

Taposiris Magna

The bedouin call it Abusir, but its ancient name must have been Taposiris, the tomb of Osiris, one of the numerous places where one of the scattered parts of the god's body was buried after its dismemberment by his brother Seth. The site is mentioned by Strabo: Taposiris, 'which is not on the sea and holds a great public festival',[48] figured in the itineraries drawn up for seafarers sailing from Alexandria to the Cyrenaica; it was known to geographers such as Pseudo-Scylax of Caryanda (around 350 BC) or Claudius Ptolemaeus (second century AD), and even appears on the *tabula Peutingeriana*, the map of the ancient world copied in 1265 from an original that must date back to the second century. Modern travellers had no difficulty identifying the place, and Napoleon's scholars made a record of its monuments in 1801.[49]

Strabo mentions a 'great public festival'. He is doubtless referring to ceremonies in honour of Osiris. The ruins of the god's temple still crown the ridge of rock that separates the lake from the sea. A large enclosure of 100 × 85 metres (110 × 93 yds), with walls 2 metres (6½ ft) thick, still rises to a height of 10 metres (33 ft); it has two pylons on the east side, inside which are staircases and service rooms. (These give an idea of what the arrangements at the Pharos would have looked like. The buildings are roughly contemporary, as the construction of the sanctuary is attributed to Ptolemy II, who inaugurated the Seventh Wonder of the World in 283.)

The temple that originally stood in the middle of this enclosure has disappeared; it was replaced by a church in the fourth century. According to travellers in modern times, it must have been of the Doric order, as is suggested by fragments of columns reused in more recent constructions inside the enclosure. At any rate, this is what Saint-Genis wrote in 1801,[50] and his statements are confirmed by the Marseillais Pascal Coste a generation later:[51] 'all the way round this ruin and in its centre one sees fragments of

The east enclosure wall of the Osiris sanctuary at Taposiris Magna, with the remains of rooms belonging to the Roman camp at its foot.

capitals, of cornices with triglyphs, fluted column drums 55 cm in diameter and other details of the Greek Doric. This supports the assumption that this building is of the Ptolemaic period.'

At the foot of the enclosure walls, one can see the ruins of a series of little rooms and also of some flights of steps which gave access to the top of the walls. These must be what is left of a Roman military camp: a transformation which numerous Egyptian temples underwent in the Roman period,[52] starting with Luxor.

The summit of the rocky ridge is occupied by the necropolis and the quarries. This soft limestone has been exploited since antiquity. The sight of the disembowelled remains of the atrium of a tomb makes one realize what damage the quarrymen have been capable of doing in the necropolis, especially in the nineteenth century. Beside simple pits the size of a man, hollowed out of the rock to a depth of around 50 centimetres (19½ in), there are also shaft graves with a square opening sunk 5 to 6 metres (c. 17 ft) down into the rock to give access to lateral chambers.[53]

The largest among these tombs have a corridor cut in the rock which leads to an atrium and to subterranean rooms, some of them very big, which contained spaces for sarcophagi which have now disappeared. It is

above a tomb of this type that a rich citizen of Taposiris had an unusual funerary monument erected. It is a replica of the lighthouse at Alexandria, and has three tiers of carefully dressed small blocks of local limestone: a square base, an octagonal section and then a cylindrical one, in the same order as the Pharos.

The whole edifice is 30 metres high (almost 100 ft), that is a fourth or fifth the size of the original. Inside, room was left for a staircase giving access to the summit. Unfortunately, the monument's poor state of preservation (it was heavily restored fifty years ago) makes it impossible to tell whether some kind of light had been installed on top of the upper tier. That said, even without a beacon, the building must have been an important landmark for sailors both on the sea and on the lake. It can be seen from a long way away on all sides. Its continuing usefulness is shown by the fact that it figures as a landmark on the charts of the British Admiralty.

Strabo says that Taposiris is 'not on the sea', which seems a paradoxical thing to say of a coastal town. It must be understood that it lies facing the lake, on the southern slope of the rocky barrier which separates the lake from the sea. Its situation here shows that its main commercial activity was concentrated on wares in transit on Lake Mariut, and also on overland routes, as we shall see.

The ruins of Taposiris, which cover more than a square kilometre, are almost completely unexcavated, apart from some limited undertakings which have remained unpublished.[54] The tops of the walls of buildings show through on the surface almost everywhere: it would be possible to draw up a plan of the town based on their alignments, before even starting to dig. The American expedition which works there also tells us in its brief report that it has uncovered a public administrative building[55] and some baths on the shore of the lake.

The lakeside here has been laid out in a remarkable way: a long break-water, rising more than 3 metres (10 ft) above the level of the lake, extends from north to south for more than 300 metres (330 yds): its northern end is joined to the southern shore by a wall which barricades the basin and prevents all movement to and fro. Boats were obliged to pass beneath a bridge which connected the breakwater to the northern shore. This arrangement obviously facilitated traffic control and tax collection.

This must have been a customs checkpoint for boats coming from or going to Alexandria, like the one at Schedia, the city's other customs har-bour, thirty kilometres (19 miles) to the east, at the point at which the canal which brought its water branched off the Nile. That Taposiris was a customs

The lighthouse of Taposiris Magna, a quarter-size replica of Alexandria's famous Pharos, is a funerary monument standing over the principal chamber of a large hypogeum of the second century BC. Like the Pharos, it has three tiers: square, hexagonal and cylindrical. It was restored after the Second World War. It was then in such a poor state of preservation that it was impossible to tell whether it had had a beacon fire. However, in its situation on top of the cliff, it certainly served as a landmark both for sailors approaching by sea and for those on the lake.

The necropolis of Plinthine: above, an unfinished Doric tomb, and, right, view of a room in a tomb with painted stelae.

station is confirmed by the existence of a long wall, known as the wall of the Barbarians, which bars the onshore route to the west of the temple of Osiris. This wall, which appears from its construction in big blocks of local limestone to be of the Hellenistic period, and of which several courses are still visible, ran from the sea to the lake and blocked the way of caravans travelling in both directions.[56]

This, then, was Taposiris' main function in antiquity: the town was a customs station where there was a police checkpoint, and where dues were levied on all the trade with the west of the country and with Cyrenaica. Clearly this trade was important enough for these measures to be worthwhile. We have seen that the countryside's fertile vineyards alone must have channelled towards Alexandria a plentiful flow of boats laden with amphorae full of wine.[57] Moreover, considering the dangers lurking on the coast, which was shallow, studded with reefs and liable to violent northerly storms,[58] it is easy to imagine that people preferred to take the much safer routes across the lake.

Plinthine and its necropolis

A kilometre east from Taposiris lie the ruins of another little Greek town, Plinthine, which occupies a prominent position on a rocky, horseshoe-shaped outcrop. Gratien Le Père describes it in his account of the region: 'I wish to speak of a fairly prominent mound which one notices on the same chain which separates the lake from the sea. On the far side of this hillock, which lies 1000 to 1200 metres from the Tower of the Arabs on the way back to Alexandria, one can just make out a kind of steps, some sections of masonry in dressed stone, finally some quadrangular, sloping surfaces which give the whole structure a pyramidical form.'[59]

Below this mound, one can, if one is on foot, trace the course of the main street through the remains visible on the surface, as it descends towards the lake; also those of other roads that run at right angles and the outlines of houses and warehouses. Here, too, the houses lie in tiers on the slope facing the lake, not the sea. The town appears to be orientated more towards the traffic on the lake than towards the sea coast.

In spite of the importance of its ruins, Plinthine has seen practically no excavations so far. However, going by the results of the investigations conducted by Adriani in 1938–9 and the work carried out by the Egyptian Archaeological Service in 1960,[60] it would be a worthwhile project. These investigations, which concern the necropolis and the Hellenistic hypogea of the second century BC, are very interesting. Firstly, the burial enclosures

In the same room, some *loculi* have been sealed with slabs painted or decorated in stucco with representations of doors and windows modelled on those of local houses of the Ptolemaic period.

(dry-stone walls separating the individual plots) are well preserved and allow us to study the way these were divided up among the dead. This is something that has not been preserved at all in the Alexandrian necropoleis. At the same time, the tombs of Plinthine provide a lot of information about the monuments that were erected over the underground tombs and marked their place in the landscape, for example those which a team of Polish archaeologists uncovered recently 100 kilometres (62 miles) west of Alexandria, at Marina el-Alamein, where pillars and columns supporting sculptures were erected above the tombs.

Among the hundred or so burials in the necropolis, four subterranean tombs are particularly well preserved. A flight of steps cut in the rock leads to an atrium, a grave shaft which provides the group of underground rooms with light. An orderly sequence of burial chambers has been cut out of the rock. These once had doors, as can be seen from the mortices of the hinges still in place; they are oblong and many of them have a bench running round the walls under the *loculi*. Some of the latter are still sealed up with slabs decorated with paintings or stucco. A beautiful *dexiosis* stele, like the one in the necropolis at Gabbari (see p. 194), has kept the freshness of its expression, while beside it a double door with a frame with Doric pilasters has been carved in stucco; it too is like the ones in the necropolis. This door faces some slabs set on edge and still pointed with mortar; they bear several dozen seal imprints with Greek names, presumably those of magistrates whose official seal guaranteed that the burial would not be disturbed. This is a procedure known from pharaonic Egypt, but I know of no other example in the country from the Graeco-Roman period.

In a neighbouring tomb, a stuccoed frame represents a monumental door with two double columns crowned with capitals of the type commonly known as 'Nabatean', but which, as one sees here, are really Alexandrian. Between these columns, two Anubises face one another, sitting on their haunches, as guardians of the dead. Above them is a band of *uraei*, or rearing cobras; and above these, Greek architectural elements – an entablature supporting a pediment.

The necropolis of Plinthine presents us with a mixture of Egyptianizing and Greek motifs, just like the Alexandrian necropoleis at the end of the Ptolemaic and the beginning of the Imperial period. This site, which has been deserted since the end of antiquity, offers a chance to study a group of tombs from which conclusions can be drawn by analogy about the devastated or entirely destroyed necropoleis of the nearby capital – about the dec-

Detail of a stele painted in gold on a white background with a frieze of dancers.

Detail of the room with a *loculus* sealed by a slab with a *dexiosis* scene: a man is clasping his wife's hand in a gesture of farewell; behind him stands a young nude boy (third century BC).

oration of the tombs, their architectural design and furnishings, and about the distribution of ownership presented on the surface by these gardens scattered with monuments erected over subterranean tombs.[61]

Philoxenite

There is another town a few kilometres south-east of Plithine, this time on the south shore of Lake Mariut. It, too, is situated in a semi-arid region and consists of a group of ruins almost untouched since the end of antiquity. Early travellers knew the site, and a team from Alexandria University has devoted several excavation campaigns to the harbour area.[62]

Here, too, one is struck by the considerable extent of the remains. All the elements of a town are there – streets, houses, public buildings – and one has the impression that, as in the case of the other two towns on the lake, simply making a record of what one can see of the courses of the walls

The monastery of St Menas was an important pilgrimage destination from the fourth to the tenth century AD. It became increasingly successful as time passed and survived for three centuries after the Arab conquest, before succumbing to attacks by the bedouin. In the 1980s, a large Coptic monastery was built in the saint's honour near the remains of the ancient one.

OPPOSITE PAGE: Relief of St Menas between his two camels. These animals are said to have knelt down by his body, which had been miraculously transported from Asia Minor, and to have refused to budge. When the body was found, people recognized this as a miracle and built a monastery on the spot to house the relics. The iconography of St Menas shows him with his camels and dressed as a Roman soldier, holding up his hands in prayer (fifth century AD).

coloured stone, which shows the care taken with the decoration of the place. The ample provision of latrines – two with a dozen places each – gives an idea of the number of visitors.

The excavations being carried out in this region continue to reveal traces of Christian occupation: for instance, some baths built of brick faced with marble have very recently been uncovered in the middle of the countryside a kilometre west of this villa. The material found there suggests a date in the fifth century. This and the following century constituted the region's *floruit*, when its prosperity depended on the stream of visitors to the great monastery nearby.

This is not the place to describe the monastery of St Menas, as it would take us too far from Alexandria; but it will have become clear from the description of the measures taken to accommodate the pilgrims going there, that it had become a very popular place to visit. Its apogee lasted for two centuries, the fifth and the sixth, and it continued to be visited into the tenth century, three centuries after the Arab conquest. The mortal remains of St Menas, a Roman soldier who became a martyr in Asia Minor, had been miraculously transported to this desert in 360; two camels had found him and refused to abandon him. This had been interpreted as a sign by the Christians of the neighbourhood and they had built a church around the saint's tomb. The fervour of which it was the object grew with his miracles – healings in particular – and soon people were coming from all over the Christian world to drink the 'water of the saint'. Thousands of 'St Menas flasks', on which the saint is represented in relief between two camels, have been found by archaeologists; they occur equally in the Necropolis and all around the perimeter of the Mediterranean, even as far away as Gaul, proving what a successful institution the monastery was.

The mystery of Marea

A mystery remains, namely the location of the town of Marea. From an examination of the ancient references to it, it seems that the site should be sought to the east of Philoxenite, nearer the canals which connect the lake with the Nile. Perhaps the archaeologists are already uncovering its remains, but, in the absence of inscriptions, without realizing it – namely in the emergency excavations in the modern town of Amareyya.

OPPOSITE PAGE: Crypt of the monastery at Abu Mina, where the saint is supposed to have been buried.

Regrets and hopes

OPPOSITE: This Hellenistic lead casing from a wooden anchor belongs to the wreckage of a ship that came from what is now the south coast of Turkey.

Fine pottery (especially oil lamps) was found in one of the wrecks discovered in 1996. Here the diver Robert Leffy has just uncovered a little bronze oinochoe.

A stone anchor has just been marked with a buoy. It will be added to the twenty or so already plotted on our map of anchors.

THE APPRAISAL OF A DECADE of rescue excavations at Alexandria has left me with a feeling of optimism, and my only regret is that I do not have more means at my disposal to respond to all the proposals of our Egyptian friends, who have faithfully maintained their confidence in us over the years.

As I have been a practising archaeologist in this city for more than twenty-five years now, I have known most of those currently in positions of responsibility, if not since they were children, then at any rate since they were young inspectors of antiquities! The adventure of the discovery of the Ptolemies' capital continues, and we – the archaeologists, the historians of Egypt and all those interested in the Graeco-Roman world – are aware that the stakes are high. This city has 'infinite variety', just like Cleopatra VII, who represents it so well. This descendant of the Macedonian royal house, who knew Egyptian as well as Greek, her mother tongue, has become the symbol of Alexandria, a veritable Isis Pharia, a Greek queen endowed with the attributes of a pharaonic divinity. She protects sailors and travellers trying to enter this difficult anchorage, with its shallow coastal waters and its reefs just beneath the surface. She offers herself as a protective deity, under the aspect not just of the mistress of the Greek city of Alexandria, but also as sovereign of all Egypt.[66]

The Alexandrian experience can also be wearisome: one has to confront various obstacles, such as the hostility of the developers who have quite other interests at heart than the enhancement of their cultural heritage. But are they any different in our own countries? When I feel exasperated (as I sometimes do) with the administrative routine, especially as I am dealing with a bureaucracy unused to the notions of emergency and rescue in a country with a civilization thousands of years old, I try to convince myself that the archaeologists who work on emergency salvage operations in European countries have exactly the same problems. The economic priorities are the same everywhere, and the frustration experienced is comparable.

So I try to keep my frustrated enthusiasm under control, until I can no longer resist the desire to enter the lists against the bulldozers to save a site which might harbour the remains of the great Library, or of the Gymnasium which excited Strabo's admiration. However, one needs energy for this kind of struggle. In spite of the time I devote to it, it is a difficult business, and often unfruitful: lack of money is going to force us to relinquish the necropolis site to the developers before we have investigated all the tombs, and they will then be destroyed in the construction of the new road.

Nonetheless, I shall conclude on a hopeful note. In spite of all the problems

posed by the safeguarding of the cultural inheritance of Alexandria in these present times, in which the archaeologists do not have nearly enough financial means at their disposal to react to the projects of the developers, and in which the awareness that irremediable losses are being sustained has not been sufficiently highlighted to prevent the destruction of remains which have miraculously survived almost until the dawn of the third millennium, all is not lost. Every excavation now under way is a challenge taken up in order to curb what could appear to be an irreversible development.

The wrecks are easy to recognize, thanks to their cargoes of wine amphorae, but normal crockery is also found in them, such as these large bowls (first century BC).

There remains one site that I have not yet discussed. In October 1996 we discovered off Qait Bey Fort a series of wrecks of Greek and Roman ships that sank within sight of Alexandria. Diving is forbidden off the Mediterranean coast of Egypt, and so their cargoes have remained in a good state of preservation. Besides numerous amphorae, some everyday pottery has been found, and also some little oil lamps and bronze vases. The ships' anchors are there too: bronze anchors or the lead casings of wooden anchors. The pottery enables us to date these cargoes and also to establish where the ships came from. One of them, for instance, dates from the sixth century AD and came from the south coast of modern Turkey.

Other, older, ships, from the third century BC, came from the island of Rhodes: their amphorae have seal imprints on both handles with the name of the owner of the vineyard and that of the priest of Helios (the Sun), after whom the current year was named in the city of Rhodos (just as it was after the consuls in Rome). It is therefore possible to date these Rhodian wrecks almost exactly to within a year. One ship came from Apulia (modern Puglia) in Italy; it had put in at one of the Cretan ports and exchanged some of its freight for a batch of amphorae of the local wine.

These ships foundered, then, even though the Pharos was operational. Strabo emphasizes the fact that the approach to the harbour was partly obstructed by reefs which were hardly visible on the surface of the water.

A diver giving a preliminary clean-up to this lead casing from a wooden anchor belonging to a wreck off Fort Qait Bey.

OPPOSITE PAGE: A wreck of a ship from Apulia in south-east Italy was full of amphorae of the Lamboglia 2 type. This picture shows a heap of their necks, still with their plugs of *pozzuolana* (volcanic ash cement).

The boats went down because they struck one of these rocky bars running parallel to the coast. They provide the archaeologists with a wealth of information about commerce between Alexandria and the rest of the Mediterranean between the fourth century BC and the seventh century AD. This new excavation covers such a large area that it will keep us busy for several years to come. Yet another new aspect of the archaeological riches of Alexandria has been revealed by this discovery.

On dry land, new opportunities to dig are becoming more numerous, and we are going to have to make some heart-rending choices. How are we to decide? We have been offered a site on Fuad Street, that is along the old Canopic Street, the great east–west axis of the city. This plot extends for about 60 metres (65 yds) from north to south, and, as the modern street is

posed by the safeguarding of the cultural inheritance of Alexandria in these present times, in which the archaeologists do not have nearly enough financial means at their disposal to react to the projects of the developers, and in which the awareness that irremediable losses are being sustained has not been sufficiently highlighted to prevent the destruction of remains which have miraculously survived almost until the dawn of the third millennium, all is not lost. Every excavation now under way is a challenge taken up in order to curb what could appear to be an irreversible development.

There remains one site that I have not yet discussed. In October 1996 we discovered off Qait Bey Fort a series of wrecks of Greek and Roman ships that sank within sight of Alexandria. Diving is forbidden off the Mediterranean coast of Egypt, and so their cargoes have remained in a good state of preservation. Besides numerous amphorae, some everyday pottery has been found, and also some little oil lamps and bronze vases. The ships' anchors are there too: bronze anchors or the lead casings of wooden anchors. The pottery enables us to date these cargoes and also to establish where the ships came from. One of them, for instance, dates from the sixth century AD and came from the south coast of modern Turkey.

Other, older, ships, from the third century BC, came from the island of Rhodes: their amphorae have seal imprints on both handles with the name of the owner of the vineyard and that of the priest of Helios (the Sun), after whom the current year was named in the city of Rhodos (just as it was after the consuls in Rome). It is therefore possible to date these Rhodian wrecks almost exactly to within a year. One ship came from Apulia (modern Puglia) in Italy; it had put in at one of the Cretan ports and exchanged some of its freight for a batch of amphorae of the local wine.

These ships foundered, then, even though the Pharos was operational. Strabo emphasizes the fact that the approach to the harbour was partly obstructed by reefs which were hardly visible on the surface of the water.

The wrecks are easy to recognize, thanks to their cargoes of wine amphorae, but normal crockery is also found in them, such as these large bowls (first century BC).

A diver giving a preliminary clean-up to this lead casing from a wooden anchor belonging to a wreck off Fort Qait Bey.

OPPOSITE PAGE: A wreck of a ship from Apulia in south-east Italy was full of amphorae of the Lamboglia 2 type. This picture shows a heap of their necks, still with their plugs of *pozzuolana* (volcanic ash cement).

The boats went down because they struck one of these rocky bars running parallel to the coast. They provide the archaeologists with a wealth of information about commerce between Alexandria and the rest of the Mediterranean between the fourth century BC and the seventh century AD. This new excavation covers such a large area that it will keep us busy for several years to come. Yet another new aspect of the archaeological riches of Alexandria has been revealed by this discovery.

On dry land, new opportunities to dig are becoming more numerous, and we are going to have to make some heart-rending choices. How are we to decide? We have been offered a site on Fuad Street, that is along the old Canopic Street, the great east–west axis of the city. This plot extends for about 60 metres (65 yds) from north to south, and, as the modern street is

narrower than the ancient one, there is a good chance that a section of the porticoes which lined it will be found here. To the north and to the south of the Shallalat Gardens, two other large sites are about to become free (one of them is a Ford garage that won a prize in an architectural competition in the 1930s). This is where the Gymnasium must have stood: the four porticoes of which it was made up measured, according to Strabo, more than a stade in length (around 180 m; *c.* 197 yds): imagine how many columns that means! Inside it were the law courts, where some famous scenes took place: it was here that the ceremony was held during which Mark Antony divided up the world between the children he had had by Cleopatra. We ought to try to start an emergency excavation here, but the size of the area is daunting and, once again, there is not enough money to see us through.

OVERLEAF: In the foreground, the neck of an amphora, and in the background a large iron anchor from a boat of the modern period, possibly the remains of an eighteenth-century vessel.

GENEALOGY OF THE PTOLEMIES

(after Michel Chauveau, *L'Égypte au temps de Cléopâtre*, Hachette Littératures, 1997)

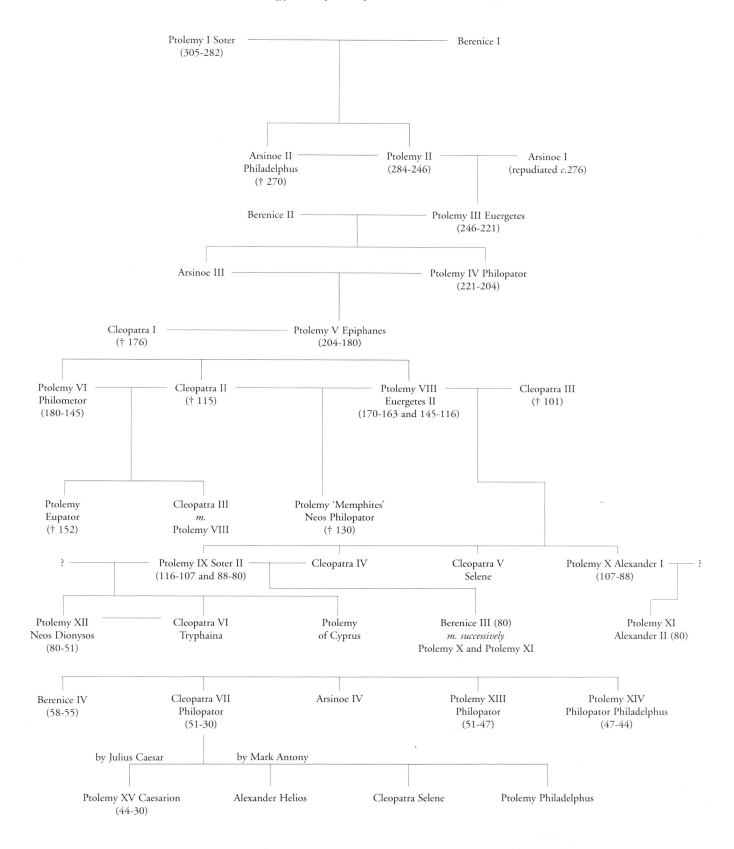

Ptolemy I Soter (305-282) — Berenice I

Arsinoe II Philadelphus († 270) — Ptolemy II (284-246) — Arsinoe I (repudiated *c.*276)

Berenice II — Ptolemy III Euergetes (246-221)

Arsinoe III — Ptolemy IV Philopator (221-204)

Cleopatra I († 176) — Ptolemy V Epiphanes (204-180)

Ptolemy VI Philometor (180-145) — Cleopatra II († 115) — Ptolemy VIII Euergetes II (170-163 and 145-116) — Cleopatra III († 101)

Ptolemy Eupator († 152)

Cleopatra III *m.* Ptolemy VIII

Ptolemy 'Memphites' Neos Philopator († 130)

? — Ptolemy IX Soter II (116-107 and 88-80) — Cleopatra IV — Cleopatra V Selene — Ptolemy X Alexander I (107-88) — ?

Ptolemy XII Neos Dionysos (80-51) — Cleopatra VI Tryphaina

Ptolemy of Cyprus

Berenice III (80) *m. successively* Ptolemy X and Ptolemy XI

Ptolemy XI Alexander II (80)

Berenice IV (58-55)

Cleopatra VII Philopator (51-30)

Arsinoe IV

Ptolemy XIII Philopator (51-47)

Ptolemy XIV Philopator Philadelphus (47-44)

by Julius Caesar — by Mark Antony

Ptolemy XV Caesarion (44-30)

Alexander Helios

Cleopatra Selene

Ptolemy Philadelphus

NOTES

CHAPTER 1
A century of archaeological research

1. Quoted in the well-documented article by M. Rodziewicz, 'Le débat sur la topographie de la ville antique', *Alexandrie entre deux mondes* (Aix-en-Provence 1987), p. 42.

2. As can be seen from the plan of the town as it was in 1865 drawn up by Mahmud el-Falaki. This peninsula was the result of silting up on either side of the Heptastadion, the causeway that connected the island of Pharos with the mainland from at least the beginning of the third century BC onwards. This is where the Ottomans installed themselves in 1517, preferring to build on this virgin soil rather than among the ruins of the Graeco-Roman city. In the nineteenth century, the city gradually grew beyond the peninsula, then experienced a period of rapid expansion from 1860 onwards. See the recent reference work on the development of Alexandria by R. Ilbert, *Alexandrie 130–1930* (Cairo 1996).

3. Mahmud el-Falaki was one of the Egyptians whom Mohammed Ali had sent to France to train as engineers. He had spent seven years at the Ecole des Arts et Métiers.

4. See M. S. Venit, 'The painted tomb from Wardian and the decoration of Alexandrian tombs', *Journal of the American Research Center in Egypt* 25 (1988), pp. 71–91, with a bibliography of earlier works on this discovery.

5. M. Sabottka, 'Ausgrabungen in der West-Nekropole Alexandrias (Gabbari)', *Die Römisch-Byzantinische Ägypten* (Mainz 1983), pp. 195–203, and 'Gabbari, 1975–1977 (Vorbericht)', *Annales du Service des Antiquités de l'Egypte* 70 (1984), pp. 277–85.

6. Besides financial support, the IFAO has provided us with considerable technical assistance, and it is a pleasure to be able to thank Nicolas Grimal, its director, without whom these excavations could not have taken place.

7. See note 2.

8. See the illustration at the top of p. 61.

9. See H. Frost, 'Alexandria: the Pharos Site', *International Journal of Nautical Archaeology* 4 (1975), pp. 126–30.

10. It is also a pleasure to thank the companies that have sponsored our work by providing material help: Leica, Zodiac and Omersub.

11. See J.-Y. Empereur, 'Les fouilles d'urgence dans la capitale des Ptolémées', *La Gloire d'Alexandrie*, exh. cat. (Paris 1998), pp. 312–20.

12. See Ahmed Abd el-Fattah and S. Ali Shoukri, 'Un nouveau groupe de tombeaux de la nécropole ouest d'Alexandrie', *Études alexandrines* 1 (IFAO 1998). See also a good presentation in A. Adriani, *Repertorio d'arte dell'Egitto greco-romano*, series C, vols i–iii (1966), nos 93–121, 129–32.

CHAPTER 2
The site of Alexandria

13. M. Chauveau, *L'Egypte au temps de Cléopâtre*, 'La Vie Quotidienne' series (Hachette 1997), p. 77.

CHAPTER 3
City walls, houses and streets

14. Strabo, *Geography* 17.1.6, trans. H. L. Jones (Heinemann 1932).

15. Plutarch, *Life of Alexander* 26.5–6, trans. Bernadotte Perrin (Heinemann 1919).

16. Diodorus Siculus 17.52.2, trans. C. Bradford Welles (Heinemann 1963).

17. *Leucippe and Clitopho* 5.1.3–4, trans. S. Gaselee (Heinemann 1917/1969).

18. Excavations of A. Adriani at the Rio Cinema; the Polish excavations at Kom el-Dikka; excavations at the former Diana Theatre.

19. M. Rodziewicz, 'Ptolemaic street directions in Basilea (Alexandria)', *Alessandria e il mondo ellenistico romano*, Congrès Alexandrie 1992 (Rome 1995), pp. 227–35.

CHAPTER 5
The Sarapeion and Pompey's Pillar

20. Tacitus, *Histories* 4.84. The Roman Aesculapius is the Greek Asklepios; Jupiter, Zeus; and Father Dis (or Pluto), Hades.

21. See F. Thélamon, 'Sérapis et le baiser du Soleil', *Antichità Altoadriatiche* 5 (1974), pp. 227–50, to whom I owe the references to Rufinus and Quodvultdeus.

22. Rufinus, *Historia Ecclesiastica* II 23.

23. Thélamon, op. cit., p. 243.

24. Pliny the Elder, *Natural History* 34.42.148, trans. H. Rackham (Heinemann 1984). The name of the architect is variously given in the manuscripts as Dinochares or Timochares.

25. Claudian, *Magnes* 5.22–39.

26. These are dowel holes used to secure the statue.

27. P.M. Fraser, *Ptolemaic Alexandria* (Oxford 1972), vol.2, p. 87.

CHAPTER 6
The Caesareum

28. *Embassy to Gaius* 151, after the translation by F. H. Colson (Heinemann 1962).

29. *Description de l'Égypte* v (1818 edn), pp. 35–42.

30. Strabo, *Geography* 17.1.27

31. See pp. 74–8 above.

32. In 1533, however, Greffin Affagart mentions only one obelisk: see p. 119.

33. Like the canal which connects Alexandria to the Nile or the 'baths of Cleopatra': see p. 131.

CHAPTER 7
A city of cisterns

34. Caesar, *Bellum Alexandrinum* 6–7, trans. A. G. Way (Heinemann 1955/1988).

35. These events took place in winter 48/47 BC.

36. Ghillebert de Lannoy (1386–1462). His work is called *Les Pèlerinages de Syrie et d'Egypte.*

37. In the month when the Nile is at its lowest, just before the flood.

38. Ghillebert de Lannoy, op. cit.

39. We have already met this '*calitz*' or *caliz* (=*khalig*) or 'canal of Cleopatra' in a quotation from Norden.

40. See the article 'Peste et croissance urbaine', by Daniel Panzat in *Alexandrie entre deux mondes* (Aix-en-Provence 1987), p. 81.

41. A French soldier employed by Mohammed Ali. He is best known for rebuilding the walls of Alexandria.

42. CEA thesis, supervised by P. Fraisse and D. Laroche (Strasbourg-Metz-Paris). Since 1996, a group of architects specializing in archaeology has been spending several months of the year on this study.

43. Excavations of Mohammed Abdel Aziz, whom I here thank for his friendly co-operation.

CHAPTER 11
The environs of Alexandria

44. Heliodorus, *An Ethiopian Story* 1.5, trans. J. R. Morgan, in B. P. Reardon (ed.), *Collected Greek Novels* (University of California Press 1989), p. 357.

45. Strabo, *Geography* 17.1.7.

46. Ibid. 17.1.4.

47. Ibid. 17.1.14.

48. Ibid.

49. May 1801: Gratien le Père, 'Mémoire sur la partie occidentale de la province de Bahyreh connue anciennement sous le nom de nome maréotique', *Description de l'Egypte, État moderne* XVIII, 2 (1823), pp. 29–57.

50. Saint-Genis, op. cit., mentions 'remains of fluted columns and Doric capitals which one finds in the ruins of the enclosure'.

51. P. Coste, *Mémoire d'un artiste. Notes et souvenirs de voyage (1815–1877)* (Marseilles 1878), I, 31.

52. *Bulletin de la Société Archéologique d'Alexandrie* 30 (1936).

53. 1905–6: excavations of E. Breccia. There is a résumé in his guidebook, *Alexandrea ad Aegyptum* (Bergamo 1914), pp. 123–30.

54. 1937–9: excavations of A. Adriani. 'Travaux de fouilles et de restauration dans la région d'Abousir', *Annuaire du Musée gréco-romain. 1940–1950*, pp.129–39. Excavations of E. L. Ochsenschjager, 'Taposiris Magna: 1975 Season', *Acts of the First International Congess of Egyptology* (Berlin 1979), pp. 503–6. A new series of excavation campaigns will be started in 1998 by an expedition of the CNRS/Université de Lyon.

55. Rather than a church, according to P. Grossmann, 'Two unusual public buildings in Abu Mina', *Alessandria e il mondo greco-romano, Alexandria 1992* (Rome 1995), pp. 178–81.

56. A. de Cosson and F. W. Oliver, 'Note on the Taenia Ridge', *Bulletin de la Société Archéologique d'Alexandrie* 32 (1938), pp. 163–76 (aerial photographs of the area between Dekhela and Taposiris: 'wall of the Barbarians' and route).

57. Amphorae workshops have been found up to sixty kilometres (37 miles) west of Alexandria.

58. See the description of a difficult journey between Alexandria and Cyrene by Synesius of Cyrene, Letter 4.

59. 'Mémoire sur la partie occidentale …' (quoted in note 47), pp. 29–57.

60. A. Adriani, 'Nécropole et ville de Plinthine', *Annuaire du Musée gréco-romain 1940–1950*, pp. 140–59, and idem, *Repertorio d'Arte* (Rome n.d.). The Egyptian excavations are unpublished.

61. O. Callot, an architect of the CNRS at the Maison de l'Orient at Lyon, has begun a study of this necropolis. His first results appear in the *Bulletin de la Sfac, Revue archéologique* (1998).

62. The excavation has remained unpublished. There is a report on it in F. el-Fakharani, 'Recent Excavations at Marea in Egypt', *Das römisch-Byzantinische Ägypten, Aegyptica Treverensia 2* (1983). pp. 175–86.

63. M. Sadak, 'The baths at the ancient harbour of Marea', *Sesto Congresso internazionale di Egittologia*, vol. I (Turin 1992), pp. 549–53.

64. M. Rodziewicz, 'Alexandria and District of Mareotis', *Graeco-Arabica* 2 (1983), pp. 199–208. He quotes the Coptic encomium, p. 202.

65. M. Rodziewicz, 'Remarks to the Peristyle House in Alexandria and Mareotis', *12. Congrès international d'archéologie classique 1983* (1988), pp. 175–8.

CONCLUSION
Regrets and hopes

66. See Irène Frain's excellent biography of the great Cleopatra VII, *L'Inimitable* (Paris 1998).

INDEX OF PERSONS, GODS AND PLACES

ILLUSTRATION CREDITS

All the illustrations are copyright Stéphane Compoint/SYGMA with the exception of the following:

Collections of the Graeco-Roman Museum, Alexandria: 18, 25, 88,
91 (photo Jean-François Gout, CEA),
93 (photo Alain Lecler, CEA),
94 right (photo Jean-François Gout, CEA),
94 left, 97 (photos Alain Lecler, CEA),
102 (photo Jean-François Gout, CEA),
125, 140, 143, 184-5 (photos Stéphane Compoint).

Jean-Yves Empereur (photos Stéphane Compoint): 19, 20, 22-3, 24, 45, 46, 49 right, 87 top, 101, 110, 111, 114, 116, 120, 123, 127, 128, 134, 152-3, 181, 214, 215.

Centre d'Etudes Alexandrines (CEA):
30, 31 (plans by Cécile Kuntz),
32 (photo Jean-Claude Hurteau),
42 (photo Alain Lecler),
44 (photo C.E. Requi),
48 (photo Alain Lecler),
50, 57 (photos Jean-Claude Hurteau),
58-9 (photo C.E. Requi),
61 top (photo Jean-Yves Empereur),

61 bottom (photos Jean-Claude Hurteau),
64, 75 bottom (photos Jean-Yves Empereur),
79 (drawing by Isabelle Hairy),
81 (photo Jean-Yves Empereur),
82, 83 (photos Alain Lecler),
87 bottom (photo André Pelle),
113 (photo Jean-Claude Hurteau),
121 (photo Jean-Yves Empereur),
129 (plan by Isabelle Hairy and Yves Guyard),
130, 131, 133, 136 (photos Jean-Yves Empereur),
144 (photo André Pelle),
155, 156, 158, 168, 169 (photos Jean-François Gout),
171, 172 (drawings by Mary-Jane Schumacher),
173 (photo Jean-François Gout),
179 (drawings by Olivier Callot),
180 (plan by Stéphane Rousseau et Thierry Gonon),
182 (drawing by Olivier Callot),
192 bottom, 201 (reconstruction by Mary-Jane Schumacher),
193 right, 195 right (reconstructions by Dorothée Kapamadijan),
213 (photo Stéphane Compoint),
216 (photo Jean-Yves Empereur),
217 (photo Alain Lecler),
219 (photo Jean-Yves Empereur),

226, 227, 228, 229, 230, 236, 237, 241, 243, 244 (photos André Pelle),
245 (photo Benoît Poinard),
246 (photo André Pelle).

Jean-Claude Golvin (watercolours): 35, 40-41, 54-5.

Mécénat technologique et scientifique d'EDF: 76, 77.

Israel Exploration Society: 96, 107.

Dagli Orti: 19, 85 top,
85 bottom (Museo della Civiltà Romana, Rome),
145 (Bibliothèque Municipale de Reims).

Mary Evans Picture Library, London: 132.

Edimedia: 115.

Photos X.D.R.: 86,
89 (Searight Collection, Victoria and Albert Museum, London),
90 (Bibliothèque Nationale de France),
95, 118, 119, 145.

First published in the United States in 1998
by George Braziller, Inc.

Originally published in France in 1998
by Librairie Arthème Fayard under the title *Alexandrie redécouverte*

French text copyright © 1998 by Librairie Arthème Fayard, Paris

Translated from the French by Margaret Maehler
English translation copyright © 1998 by The Trustees of the British Museum

For information, please address the publisher:
George Braziller, Inc.
171 Madison Avenue
New York, NY 10016

A catalog card number for this title is available from the Library of Congress.

Printed and bound in France

First edition